THE NHS
HEALER

THE NHS HEALER

How My Son's Life Inspired a Healing Journey

by Angie Buxton-King

First published in Great Britain in 2004 by
Virgin Books Ltd
Thames Wharf Studios
Rainville Road
London
W6 9HA

A catalogue record for this book is available from the
British Library.

ISBN 1 85227 179 5 *NE 9335*

Typeset by Phoenix Photosetting, Chatham Kent
Printed and bound in Great Britain by
CPD Wales

This book is dedicated to Sam and Nick, my beloved boys.

To Sam for your courage, strength, wisdom and inspiration, and to Nick for your support and understanding.

All my love, always and forever.

Mummy x

ACKNOWLEDGEMENTS

To Grazie for your love and support, and for sharing your life with me. To Alan and Angie for welcoming me with love into their family. To David for being a brilliant father to our boys. To Anthea, Denise, Hessie and Jane for their quiet support along the way. To Matt and his family, Themis and Paul, Linda, Eddie, Katie, Emma and all my patients, past and present, who have allowed details of their journeys to be used in this book. Special thanks to Stephen Rowley and all the staff on the Haematology Unit at University College London Hospital, for their support and open minds that have enabled their patients to benefit from healing. To all the dedicated staff at Great Ormond Street Hospital, who helped Sam so much during those early days. To Liz Puttick (my agent) who recognised that Sam's story deserved to be heard, Kirstie Addis for her editorial guidance, and to Virgin who have now helped my family for the third time!

FOREWORD

University College London Hospital's haematology unit treats patients with leukaemia and other life threatening diseases. These treatments are highly intensive and carry risks of morbidity and mortality in themselves. For the last five years the unit has developed a complementary therapy team, initially providing conventional therapies such as reflexology and aromatherapy to patients. Introducing a spiritual healer into this pressure cooker environment was considered a risk.

All of the healing on the unit is provided by Angie Buxton, who is now an integral member of the medical and nursing team and I am pleased to say that, over the last four years that Angie has been in the team, the therapy of healing has become not only accepted, but also imperative to many of our patients. Although, clinically, healing remains little understood, the clinical effects are most evident and certainly tangible enough to satisfy the sceptical minds of doctors and nurses. We have seen patients with uncontrolled pain find more relief from healing than intramuscularly opiates; we have seen patients in psychological states of utter desperation find, in healing, huge comfort and coping abilities; we have seen patients report significant reductions in chemotherapy-related side effects; we have seen the positive effect healing can have on the troubled dying patient. Working in this field is demanding and many staff have felt the need for healing themselves and have found significant benefit from doing so. Healing is the most popular and well-received complementary therapy we provide on the unit.

Stephen Rowley
Clinical Nurse/Manager, UCLH

PREFACE

In writing this book I hope to be able to offer hope and encouragement to anyone who has to struggle with what may seem to be a hopeless or difficult life situation. I hope that as you read this book you will begin to share my passion for the therapy of *healing*. I have come from the depths of despair following my youngest son Sam's diagnosis of leukaemia, to where I am now, working as the only paid healer within the NHS today. By writing this account of Sam's fight for life and what resulted from it I hope to show you that the tools we used to help Sam are available to us all.

Many people now realise that we cannot just rely upon conventional medicine to hold the answer to all our problems, and the general public are voting with their feet and accessing complementary therapies in ever increasing numbers. We as patients and carers should ask for these therapies to be made available to us from our hospitals and GP surgeries. I have seen for myself the power of the patient to bring about changes within the NHS. We can all play our part in asking for these therapies to be made available to us.

In writing this book I have shed many tears, but I hope you will see how healing worked for Sam and I hope you will feel uplifted by the quality of life he and our family enjoyed. In the case studies, you will see how healing has helped many people with different types of health and emotional problems, and I hope you will begin to see how healing may be able to help you whatever your problem is. I hope that Sam's story will help you to find courage for yourself and your family if you are facing illness or the potential loss of a loved one, whether it is a child, a spouse or a dearly loved parent or friend.

My experience has been that no belief system is necessary for healing to be of benefit. In my own case I build my beliefs on what I have actually had proven to me or seen with my own eyes. Whether we label healing as spiritual healing, Reiki, therapeutic touch or any other name, I believe it is simply the channelling of love and energy. My belief as a healer is that we have physical bodies that are surrounded by energy bodies. When we are ill – emotionally, physically, or mentally – these energy bodies become unbalanced. A healer has the ability to channel energy and will be able to assist in the rebalancing of the energy bodies, which will in turn have a beneficial effect on the physical body. Patients will often comment on feeling more balanced and more energetic after a treatment. This is, of course, a simplistic explanation but one that I have seen validated on numerous occasions. As for my beliefs on God I have yet to meet or see him so I am undecided. However, I believe we come from somewhere and return to somewhere. I refer to this place as *spirit*; I believe it is our spirit or soul that is eternal and continues to live after our physical bodies are dead.

I have been lucky enough since Sam's death to meet a wonderful medium who has the ability to communicate with spirit, and I have been given countless examples of Sam's continuous existence, hence my belief that life is eternal and love is the binding key. This is what I believe at the time of writing, but my heart and mind remain open to new information as I become convinced of it. I do not believe that blind faith helps me personally but I respect and honour the beliefs of others.

I hope to encourage any healers who are reading this book to see that we *do* make a difference to our patients and we can and do work alongside conventional medicine successfully. I want you to feel motivated to approach the hospital that you would like to work in. Hopefully, I will then no longer be in the unique position of being the only paid healer working within the NHS, but just one of many making a difference to patients and staff in this setting.

To any sceptics reading this book I would ask that you do what staff at University College London Hospital have done – try it for yourself and then judge its effectiveness by how you or your patients benefit. Science can at present not fully explain the process, but that doesn't make the benefits of healing any less real. Go on – try it!

PROLOGUE

In 1995 my youngest son Sam was diagnosed with Acute Myeloid Leukaemia (AML). He was seven years old. Worse was to come – the tests that he subsequently took showed that he had the most difficult type of leukaemia. Acute Myeloid Leukaemia is a form of cancer that affects blood-producing cells in the bone marrow; the disease mainly affects the white-cell production in the bone marrow.

In general there are seven subtypes of AML and further tests would show that Sam had the least common, affecting approximately 15 per cent of children who are diagnosed with leukaemia. The statistics suggested that Sam's subtype did not respond well to treatment. I was plunged into the fear that is every parent's nightmare, the potential loss of my child. My fear was compounded by the fact that my mother had died of ovarian cancer in 1988 (the year that Sam was born). Having seen her suffer, the thought of my beautiful child having to do the same was almost unbearable. My instinct was to pick Sam up and run. I wanted to get as far away as I could from Great Ormond Street Hospital, where we were being treated.

Once the initial shock of diagnosis had abated I began to feel more optimistic. Yes, Mum had died but I knew so much more now. I had become very interested in *healing* as a therapy and had become very aware that there is so much more to health than just curing the physical body. I felt that with a combination of both conventional and complementary therapies we could help Sam to be well again.

That belief took us as a family on an adventure during which we left no stone unturned to help Sam.

Sam was amazing from day one; his courage and positive outlook were an inspiration to everyone who met him on the roller coaster that was our life for the next three years.

The doctors continued to warn us that the chances were not high that Sam would respond to treatment. They were right in some ways; Sam's initial treatment had lasted eight months and it had often been very difficult for the whole family emotionally, but remarkably he had suffered far less physically than many of his peers at Great Ormond Street. I believe this was due to the healing he received on a regular basis. Every day with Sam was a gift and when he died, he did so peacefully at home having lived every day of his life to the full.

Having seen at first hand what healing could achieve for Sam – fewer side effects from toxic treatments, less pain, more positivity, more quality of life – I wanted to offer those same qualities to other patients.

During the four years that I have worked at University College London Hospital (UCLH), the healing service has steadily expanded to the current four days a week. This is as a direct result of how popular the therapy of healing is; one day a week was no longer enough to see all the patients who found healing an invaluable tool while they were undergoing their rigorous chemotherapy protocols. It is wonderful that the healing is available more often as the more healing a patient receives in this setting the better the results will be.

It is a great sadness to me that more hospitals do not offer the wonderful complementary care that UCLH does. I very much hope that other hospitals will do so in the future, opening their doors to healers and other therapies. However, in the past few months I have begun to receive referrals from the paediatric oncology (children's cancer) unit within our trust. This is an area of work that is very close to my heart as I have seen at first hand the benefits that can be achieved for children undergoing chemotherapy through Sam's journey.

Recently I was asked to see a child who had a great fear of

needles. When I arrived on the ward I could hear a child screaming and it soon became evident that this was who I was coming to see. The doctor was in the middle of trying to insert a canular (intravenous needle) and the whole family were extremely distressed. I had not met the child before but his mother saw that I had arrived and asked me to come in and help in whatever way I could.

The child was about ten – the same age as Sam when he passed into spirit – and I was immediately struck by how similar in appearance they were. He looked up at me with tears in his eyes and I felt a huge flood of understanding pass between us; it was as if he knew that I could help in some way. I took a deep breath to steady myself, explained very briefly what I was going to do and then laid my hands on his head to begin the healing. I was aware of very strong energy flowing through me and, as I glanced over my shoulder, I could see the child's vein plump up and the needle go in without him even noticing. The whole procedure was over in moments and the doctor and nurse looked at me in amazement, saying, 'Nice trick. How did you do that?' It is actually a very simple explanation. The energy relaxes the body; consequently, veins that had constricted with the child's fear dilate with the relaxation response.

Since then I have been asked to see several children to help them with similar situations and each time I am reminded of how effective healing is in this setting and how brave Sam was and how brave these children are. They deserve all the help we can offer them and the paediatric oncology unit is now in the process of looking into having a healer available for their patients. Working with these children is one of the most fulfilling things I can do – every time I work with a child Sam comes sharply into focus and I am aware that I am getting closer to what I really need to be doing: spreading the therapy of healing throughout cancer services and not just being content with what has been achieved so far.

I hope this book will offer you resources and self-help tools that will make your personal journey more comfortable. We hold inside ourselves valuable information on how to heal ourselves – we just need help to unlock this information. This information, combined with conventional medicine when necessary, could unlock the door to your new future. Please remember that whatever your problem is and however hopeless the medical prognosis sounds, your life is there to be lived and in the absence of anything else there is nothing wrong with hope. It is hope that will give you the quality of life that we as a family enjoyed with Sam.

CHAPTER 1

We were a very normal family of four – Mum, Dad, Nick and Sam. David and I had been married for fifteen years, and we had always considered ourselves fortunate to have enough money to get by, which allowed me to stay at home and bring up the children. Most of all we were all blessed with our health. I would tell the boys, when they wanted something we couldn't afford, that there was no more important thing in life than your health.

From time to time during our marriage, I would have an overwhelming sense of fear for our future and as the years went past this fear seemed to be somehow centred on Sam. I had no real reason to feel as I did, and I would push the feeling away and try to tell myself it was just one of those morbid fears that people had sometimes, and not to be so silly.

My only experience of real sorrow had been the death of my mother at the age of 53. She had been diagnosed with ovarian cancer shortly after I became pregnant with Sam and, after a horrific struggle, she passed away three months after Sam was born in 1988. I thought my heart would break and I clung on tightly to my boys, especially Sam, during those first agonising months of grief. I used to think I had been given Sam to ease the pain of losing Mum. Although Mum's illness was terminal from diagnosis we had explored some alternative treatments, one of which was attending the Bristol Cancer Centre where she received healing amongst other complementary therapies. Mum enjoyed the healing so much that I arranged for her to have a healer call at home, so that she could have more treatments as and when she wished. It was while I was with Mum on one of these occasions that I felt myself get extremely hot and my hands began to tingle. After the session had finished I asked the healer what this meant. He smiled and said it was common for people who had the ability to channel energy to have this experience; he mentioned that I might want to explore the idea at some later date. After Mum died I read many, many books on healing; I was also very interested in mediums who communicated with our loved ones in spirit. Eventually I felt I had enough knowledge to attend a self-development group where we explored healing and psychic matters.

By the time Nick was twelve and Sam seven, my fears for the future had been put aside. Occasionally I would look at Sam and worry about him as he was such a gentle soul. I would fret that he needed to be tougher to survive in this world but there was no indication health-wise of what was to come.

As a family we enjoyed going on long bike rides and on one particular occasion during half-term holidays in October 1995, Sam complained of a bad headache and feeling breathless. I thought it might be a touch of asthma and I made a mental note to get him checked at the doctor's the following week. For no real reason I felt very uneasy – much as I had done before Mum had been taken ill – but I encouraged Sam to carry on with the bike ride and we completed it with no further mishap.

The following week David had to fly to Gibraltar on business and Sam and Nick went back to school. During the week Sam looked a little pale and I was glad that I had managed to get an appointment with our doctor for that Thursday. He could find nothing obviously wrong, saying that any problems were probably being caused by a virus. Our GP had always been very thorough, however, and this occasion was no different – he said he could arrange a blood test if it would make me feel happier. My stomach did a flip but I felt that intuitively we should have a blood test and arranged the appointment for the following day.

Sam found school difficult and I used to attend assembly to give him moral support. The next morning Jane, a friend, and I were watching the boys in morning assembly. As I looked at Sam sitting next to Jane's son Tom, I could see that he really did look a lot paler than his peers. I turned to Jane and said without knowing where the words were coming from, 'Please, please don't let it be leukaemia.' She looked at me stunned but we both knew at that moment that it was true. I really don't know what made me say those words, maybe it was motherly instinct, I don't know for sure. I'm aware that many mothers have experienced similar feelings for their children or close loved ones that they can't explain. I feel it is an ability we can tap into that can help us, almost like an inner voice that we would do well to listen to.

I spent the rest of the day pushing the terrible thought aside, and picked the boys up from school to take Sam for the pre-arranged blood test. It wasn't very pleasant but Sam soon forgot it and we went off to town for a pizza as a reward for being so brave. We arrived home in good spirits to find our doctor waiting for us. I knew at once why he was there and asked the boys to go off and play while I talked to the doctor. I have no idea why the blood test was looked at so swiftly – maybe the hospital had a policy with children to speed it through, but whatever the reason the results were available within a few hours.

As our GP and I walked into the lounge I could feel the blood rushing through my ears and head, and we both sat down. He must have thought me deranged as I turned to him and said, 'OK, tell me what it is and then we can get on and fight it.' The fight for Sam had begun.

CHAPTER 2

The boys came downstairs wanting to know what the doctor had to say. I pulled myself together as quickly as I could and tried to mask my shock, simply saying that Sam had very sick blood and would need to have very strong medicine in hospital to fix it. Sam had to go to our local hospital the next day prior to going to Great Ormond Street Hospital. Sam and Nick were initially very shocked and we huddled together on the sofa. I hugged them both close, reassuring Sam that at no time would he be left alone and either David or myself would be with him while he was in hospital.

We all cried together for a while and then the boys went off to play on the computer (such is the resilience of children). I rang my mother-in-law Pat, who lived just around the corner; she in turn rang a good friend of mine and then came around to the house straightaway. Pat was always very stoic in times of trouble and she remained calm during that night and the following terrible day.

David worked for a company that sent him overseas frequently and he was still away on business. I tried repeatedly to ring him in Gibraltar but was unable to contact him, finally reaching him in the early hours of the morning. Telling him over the phone that the doctor had said we might lose Sam was awful and I can only guess at the anguish he must have gone through that night alone in his room. There were no flights available until later on the next day, so we had to carry on at home without him.

My close friends Denise and Hester came to the house and we all sobbed together. Hester and Denise had the unenviable task of ringing people and telling them what was going on. I'm sure it was a terrible evening for a lot of people receiving the news – it was, after all, every parent's nightmare – but this time it wasn't somebody else's family, it was mine.

Looking around me I could see that I had much to do if I was going to be ready for a stay in hospital the next day. Hoovering and ironing kept me busy well into the night but eventually I collapsed into bed. Since Pat was staying in Sam's room, he was staying in my bed. I spent the night hugging him and looking at his small vulnerable face as he slept peacefully. I could not believe looking at him, that there really was this terrible illness at work in his small body. The shock took hold of me and I ran to the bathroom and vomited as if trying to purge myself of this terrible news. I lay awake that night while the boys slept peacefully and as morning approached I began to feel stronger. I thought to myself, 'I've already lost Mum, I'm not losing Sam too.' I was comforted by the fact that I knew how to give healing to Sam and was convinced this would help him.

The boys awoke normally the following day, they both ate breakfast and we set about packing a bag with provisions for the day. Essentials such as Game Boy machines to keep them amused, drinks and food, and most importantly Sam's cuddly white teddy bear. The boys seemed quite normal with no outward signs of distress. We arrived at our local hospital to find the paediatric consultant waiting for us; she had obviously been alerted by our GP. We were shown into a single room and told that a nurse would be in shortly to take some blood for more tests.

Sam and Nick were very happy to find that we had our own room – neither of them were particularly sociable children. We had brought the Mega Drive machine with us and our room had its own TV. This meant that we were able to set up our games machine and make our own private space, which suited us perfectly. Pat had come with us and had brought snack foods and cartons of orange juice that, months previously, David had brought back from a trip to Romania. It was only when Pat started to look quite merry that we realised what was in them – orange and vodka! Just as well we hadn't offered any to the boys. Despite our worrying situation we found the fact that we were drinking vodka and orange at a time like this very amusing – as did the boys!

The nurse arrived and Sam held out his arm quite happily for the needle, but four attempts later he was distraught and so was I – it was proving very difficult to get into a vein. Pat took Nick outside as he was becoming distressed watching his brother suffer. After a lot of tears the sample was finally taken and we comforted Sam and waited for the results.

The consultant had meanwhile talked to Pat, and had told her much the same as our GP had said the previous day. Sam had Acute Myeloid Leukaemia and there was very little hope. We found out later that, understandably, neither our GP nor the consultant were experts in the field of childhood leukaemia, but were trying to give us the best of their general knowledge. No paediatric consultant in a general hospital could be expected to have the expertise that a consultant specialising in the field of childhood leukaemia would have. They were out of date regarding the latest treatments that could be offered, and they had both given us a much worse picture than they should have done at that point. The consultant spoke to me later and said the new tests confirmed that Sam had AML and she did not expect him to respond to treatment. She had spoken to Great Ormond Street Hospital and they had a bed arranged for the following morning. She was reluctant to let us go home until she had spoken to David, but when I explained that he was en route from Gibraltar, she relented and agreed we would be better off at home for the night.

The boys had by now fully recovered from the ordeal of the blood test and were yelling for burgers and drinks. I took Nick out to the local shops to search for food while Pat stayed with Sam. While we were out Nick asked me why I was crying so much. I tried to explain to him how it felt to be a mother and to have a child that was very ill. We talked about leukaemia and what the treatment would involve and he asked me what would happen if the treatment didn't work. I told him truthfully that some children did die from this illness, but Sam was most definitely not going to die. I said that

I believed Sam was going to get better even though it might take a long time. Nick accepted this news with no more comment than 'well, in that case, please stop crying'. Good advice – which I'm afraid I wasn't able to follow for quite some time. We returned to the ward to find David's sister Anthea, who had arrived with bags of goodies to cheer the boys up. She was a breath of fresh air coming into the hospital, treating Sam completely normally, which enabled us to calm down.

David arrived home later that day and we were all relieved to see him; he was the missing piece of our personal jigsaw and we all felt stronger now he was home again. Amazingly the rest of that day was spent as a normal family, the last day that would be normal for us for a long while to come. The boys went to bed at their usual time and it was only then that David and I allowed ourselves to cry together for the desperate plight of our son.

Those times that we had lain in bed thinking how lucky we were had come back to haunt us, and the unspoken fear was now a reality. David never really spoke to me about how he felt at that time. I think the fear for both of us was so overwhelming that it robbed us of any ability to communicate with each other. I didn't realise at the time that this inability to communicate would be something that would have a negative effect on our lives in the future.

CHAPTER 3

As we drove down to London the next morning, my mind was filled with a million different thoughts of all the people I felt I needed to contact and things I needed to do. In a way I felt that everything I had learned through Mum's illness was going to help us as a family now. It was almost as if my whole life had been leading up to this moment.

First on my list of things to do was to set up some absent healing for Sam. I believed from my experience with Mum that we would need to use more than just strong drugs to help Sam get well. I knew I could help Sam by giving him regular healing but I wanted as many people as possible to be sending healing to him. Absent healing is very similar to prayer in that the more people who are thinking of Sam and sending positive thoughts for his recovery the better. Mum's experience at the Bristol Cancer Centre showed me the importance of a holistic approach to illness and I knew that, even though Sam was a child, it would also be important for him. I wanted to make sure we would use everything in our power to help him get well.

We arrived in London and parked in a back street close to the hospital. As we walked into the famous entrance my mind went numb but I put on a cheerful face for the boys' sake. Seeing the words Oncology and Bone Marrow Transplants next to our floor was another blow to the senses. We left the lift and followed the 'robin' footprints on the floor leading to our ward. We did not know then that Robin Ward was to be our home for the next eight months.

Our room was a huge relief to us as it was fitted out with a sofa bed for parents to stay, and our own bathroom. In addition, the curtains on the corridor side were greatly appreciated as we could close them and thereby shut out the rest of the world when we needed some privacy. One of the great perks for Sam was that the room had its own TV and video, which meant of course that he could play computer games to his heart's content.

Sam later told me that when he entered the hospital he wondered if he would ever leave there but, when he saw his room and met the nurse who was to look after us that day, he knew that he would be fine.

The doctors arrived to check Sam over and seemed very surprised that he looked so fit and well. They arranged to insert a cannula – a single intravenous needle – into Sam's arm. This would alleviate the need for repeated needles while he was undergoing the tests they needed to run.

Sam had a haemoglobin blood count that morning of 6.9 – a normal count for a child is over 11.0, so he needed a blood transfusion quite quickly. The cannula was fitted and Sam was hitched up to the electronic machine that would pump the blood into him, which we christened Fanny. He very quickly became used to being attached to Fanny and was moving around the room within a short space of time. I think it was more of a blow to David and me as we could see all the other bare-headed little children on the ward dragging their pumps around and we knew that very soon Sam would look just like they did. The large stone in my chest that had once been my heart grew heavier.

The doctors had arranged for a bone marrow test to be done to ascertain which type of AML Sam had so that they would have a clearer idea of the treatment they would be offering us. They commented again on how well Sam was and said that most children were very ill by the time they reached Great Ormond Street, as blood tests were often not given until the child had been ill for some months and had got weaker and weaker from repeated infections. We were so lucky that our GP had suggested a blood test and I will always be thankful for the head start it gave us.

Robin Ward is a purpose-built ward and has very good facilities, including a kitchen for parents' food and a separate kitchen for the children with very strict hygiene rules for when the children became neutropenic (chemotherapy is used in the fight against leukaemia and neutropenia is a side effect of the treatment when your bone marrow function falls below a certain level – neutropenia means that your body has no resistance to infections).

There was a separate shower room for parents and of course the nurses' station and rest room. David commented that it was like joining a very select club, but one in which no one wanted to be a member. The children's food came up on a separate trolley and Sam quickly pronounced it inedible. I resolved to bring fresh food in for him so he would have no excuse not to eat. As time went on I was grateful for Sam to eat whatever he would agree to, which sometimes was burgers obtained from the nearest Burger King. As often as I could manage, however, I cooked dinners in the parents' kitchen or brought ready-cooked meals in from home.

A bone marrow aspirate test was performed that afternoon; it would be the first of many such tests that Sam would have to endure. This would give them much more detail than a normal blood test – as well as showing which subtype of AML Sam had, it would also give information of any chromosome abnormalities that may have been present that would affect the treatment Sam would undergo. He was sedated with a drug called ketamine, which meant that he was not unconscious, but in a heavily drugged state. This would enable the doctors to obtain the sample and then Sam would quickly come round again.

David and I were able to stay with Sam while he drifted off and it was like watching a small animal being put to sleep – we both went outside and howled. The procedure only took a few minutes and then David carried Sam back to our room. Sam came around very quickly and he and Nick were soon playing happily on the Mega Drive – it took a lot longer for David and myself to recover.

The haematology registrar confirmed the diagnosis of AML, but further results to establish the subtype would not be ready for about a week. The good news was that Sam had no blast cells in his central nervous system (blast cells are immature cells that look abnormal) but the bad news was that he had approx 85 per cent blast cells in his bone marrow. This was a very high level – a normal marrow in remission from leukaemia would show less than 5 per cent blast cells. We were given a leaflet on a new trial that was being run to test one drug against another. We were sent away to read the leaflet and then decide what we wanted to do. It didn't feel much of a choice: one drug damaged the heart and the other was being trialled to see if it was any less damaging. I feel very strongly that to be asked to make decisions about drugs with only an information leaflet for guidance is very wrong. I'm sure that this is the only way trials can be conducted ethically, but it is very difficult to make these judgments when you are a layman in medical terms. We were lucky in that our neighbour at home had access to an expert in the same field and was able to advise us a little. However, the decision was still ours and we made our choice. We were then told that a computer would make the final decision, which is apparently the normal way of conducting these trials. I was very upset that after making our choice there was really no choice, as the computer had the last word. As it turned out, we were chosen to follow the regime that we had wanted, but I couldn't help but imagine the extra worry if we had not.

During that first consultation I asked whether we had any choice other than to follow the chemotherapy protocols, and mentioned alternatives. They said that they had no real knowledge of anything other than chemotherapy being effective but had no objection to me using healing alongside their protocols. David and I discussed our choices and decided to go ahead with the chemotherapy as we felt we had to place our trust in conventional medicine. David had no real belief that what I was doing with healing would be of any help, but he felt I could do no harm and so was happy for me to arrange whatever I thought would benefit Sam.

We were lucky to have a parent to look after each child; I often wonder how we would have managed if we had more children. Nick had always been very close to David and went home with him, seemingly not worried about the separation from Sam and myself.

After they had left for home Sam and I settled down for the night and I wrote a few letters to some close friends.

I don't remember what I wrote but one of my friends later told me that my grief was palpable and she had to put the letter down several times as she got so upset reading it. The mask had been firmly in place all day but when I began to write, all my grief and emotions came pouring out. Sam slept peacefully on and I stood watch over him for some time, placing my hands on his body to channel healing into him. I did this in the most simple and basic way that I had learned during my mother's illness. Taking a few deep breaths I imagined a bright stream of light coming down from above, entering my head and down through my body, arms and hands into Sam.

He didn't stir as I gently touched him where I felt he needed help most: his head to help him cope with the momentous changes going on in his young life, and his heart to give him strength.

The nurses came in and out of the room during the night, taking Sam's blood pressure and checking his blood transfusion was going through without any problems. It is difficult to sleep with nursing staff doing their duties, so I spent the rest of the night reading all there was to read about AML and making a list of people I felt I needed to contact.

I had a list of healers from when Mum was ill that I wanted to try and contact, and all the reading I had done in the past seven years had given me lots of ideas of other complementary therapies that I also wanted to explore. Firstly there was the absent healing mentioned earlier, then I wanted to contact someone who practised with Bach flower remedies, as I had read they were very helpful for the emotions. I was also very interested in radionics, which could be used to help combat some of the side effects of treatment.

I wanted to access as much help as I could. David and I had very little time to discuss anything at this time, as we were too busy making arrangements for Nick and Sam to spend any time talking to each other, but we were lucky to have a very strong family unit, one in which our only concern was to help Sam get well again. Nick said very little about how he felt, only saying some years later that he accepted Sam was very sick but hoped that the medicine would help him get better again.

Some people might find this attitude strange but children are very accepting of changing circumstances and we all deal with things in our own way. Over the years I have learned that there are no right or wrong ways to cope with situations such as this; it is down to the dynamics of each individual family to cope in the way that suits them best. David and I were handling things very differently, but the overall effect at the time was a united front to help Sam as much as we could.

CHAPTER 4

David and Nick arrived back at the hospital the next morning as planned. Nick had not wanted to go to school and who could blame him? I could identify completely that he wanted to be with us and to know what was happening.

The family in the next room had a little boy of five called Harry, who also had AML. Unfortunately this was the second hospital admission for Harry as he had been treated successfully earlier in the year for his leukaemia. He had been in remission (when the symptoms of a disease abate to a low level) but had now relapsed and had returned. His mum and dad, Jane and John, were in no mood to communicate when we first met them, but as time passed we exchanged war stories and Jane was to become a great source of information to us. It was proving difficult to get Harry back into remission and so the doctors were trying a new form of treatment called FLAG (a name made up from an abbreviation of the names of the four drugs within the treatment protocol) and, if that were successful, they would be having a bone-marrow transplant with Harry's sister as the donor. Since our aim was also to get to a point where we could consider a bone-marrow transplant for Sam, any information Jane and John could give us was useful.

Our first full day at Great Ormond Street passed for us with a huge amount of people coming in and out of our room offering help and information. Unfortunately we found the amount of help completely overpowering, and when the hospital teacher arrived to say hello to Sam, it was just about the last straw! Sam wasn't happy at school anyway and he was horrified to think he had to do school work here – he burst into tears. We asked the teacher to leave and not return until invited and closed our door firmly. This may sound a bit harsh as the teacher was only doing her job, but the timing was not right for us, especially as we weren't in the room with Sam when she called. We had been taken into a side room to talk to the consultant about Sam's treatment and returned to find him in tears.

Our next visitor was a nurse who took care of the Hickman lines. A Hickman line is a flexible double plastic tube that is inserted into the wall of the chest under the arm, then fed into a main artery. It delivers all the chemotherapy, drugs and medicines via the heart to the bone marrow. The nurse had a book, which explained the device, and various pictures to illustrate how it all worked. Sam was reasonably happy to let her sit down and explain 'the line' until she reached a page that showed a small boy of Sam's age with a Hickman line fitted with absolutely no hair on his head at all. Sam sobbed until he fell asleep with exhaustion. We had explained that he would lose his hair but to see such graphic pictures really upset him. While we needed to know about Hickman lines I thought the picture was unnecessary. All of the nurses were excellent and doing their best for our children, but we weren't the only family to find the pictures difficult and I believe that since then some changes have taken place to make them more child friendly.

Sam's operation to insert the line was scheduled for the following morning. In the reception area of the ward was a pool table and the boys spent the afternoon playing – they seemed happy enough. Considering that we had only arrived the previous day I was very proud of the way both boys had adjusted. It was a small indicator of Sam's amazing willpower and strength of character that would carry him though the coming treatment.

I spent the time going in and out of the bathroom trying to conceal my tears from Sam and Nick, and David made endless cups of coffee for us both; neither of us could eat as swallowing food had become impossible. We still didn't talk to each other; our pain was so clearly mirrored in each other's eyes that we would have broken down if we had talked. We concentrated on the boys' needs first as we always had done in our relationship.

Once Sam had the Hickman line in place the chemotherapy infusions were scheduled to begin. A nurse came into our room to explain the protocol and the side effects of the drugs. She explained that once Sam was receiving chemotherapy his urine would have to be collected by us for the staff to monitor his output, and for our protection we would have to use disposable gloves. This really brought home to me how toxic the chemotherapy would be – to think that this medicine that I had to protect myself from was going directly into my son's blood was horrific.

During the day I had made various calls from the phone in the corridor outside our room, one of them to a local healer in St Albans. I briefly told her our situation and arranged to see her that evening. Nick and I set off for home, leaving David to spend the night at the hospital with Sam. It gave Nick and myself a chance to talk and he asked a few questions which I answered honestly. The hospital had wanted us to tell Sam everything about his illness and the possibility of him dying. I totally disagreed with them and did not – and still do not – think it is appropriate for a small boy to be weighed down with the enormity of life and death. I had told Sam that some children became very ill indeed but that he would get better although sometimes the medicine would make him feel very sick and low. If I believed as I did and still do that positive thoughts were of vital importance to getting him well, how could I possibly feed him negative ideas? The staff were all made aware of our feelings on the matter and most of the time dealt with Sam in a positive way.

I met with the healer Jean Galbraith that evening, leaving Nick in Pat's care. Jean had endured a terrible few years herself, losing both her daughter and then her husband, but she showed me nothing but love and compassion. By the time I left her, I felt that I had tapped into something that would sustain not only Sam but myself as well. I intended to try and arrange some healing for myself as soon as possible. I had offered the chance of healing to both David and Nick, who would not agree to receive any healing then, but reasoned that if I was strong and well that would help us all and healing was an important part of that. It was not that David didn't agree with healing, he just didn't want to access it for himself at that point.

I also saw a homeopath that same evening and she spent a long while listening to me and building up a picture of Sam. She subsequently sent us a homeopathic remedy after consulting with a colleague who was experienced in helping cancer patients. Sam took this alongside his conventional treatment. She recommended a book by an American oncologist, Bernie S. Siegel, called *Love, Medicine and Miracles*. The book was to be a great source of information and inspiration to me, which I read over and over in those first few weeks.

There were masses of messages on our answering machine when Nick and I returned home that first evening, but I found it impossible to talk to people at that time. That would come later.

CHAPTER 5

The following morning I took Nick to school as normal. He needed to get back into a routine to enable him to cope with the upheaval in our lives. We were lucky to have Pat living close by which made arranging care for Nick, when David and I were both at the hospital, relatively easy. We had been offered help from various sources so that Nick would not have to come to the hospital every evening after school, but Nick said he would prefer to come home and then travel up to London to see Sam whenever he could. I also felt it was important for Nick that he was as involved with developments as much as possible.

I drove back down to London to find Sam in very good spirits. He had met a nurse named Stephen the night before who had encouraged him to come out of his room and have a game of pool. Stephen also introduced Sam into the dubious world of water fights using 50ml syringes! Stephen was to become a great friend to us all, lifting Sam's spirits and giving us as much information as we asked for – a great ally to have.

Our consultant, on the other hand, was no doubt a brilliant doctor and scientist but he had one major fault as far as I was concerned. He dealt only in statistics and protocols and seemed to have no concept of giving hope and encouragement to the parents.

He explained the various subtypes of AML to us and repeated that he would not get the results of the bone-marrow aspirate test for a further week. The treatment was the same for all AML cases in the early stages of treatment, however, so they would start the first course of chemo that night. It would be the first of possibly four or five courses and he told us that we should prepare ourselves for a stay of six months or more.

We returned to our room and tried to calm ourselves, as we had to take Sam down to the operating theatre for them to fit his Hickman line. Sam had decided that he did not want to go to theatre on a trolley but wanted to walk down, so David and I walked down with him holding a hand each. It was one of the worst experiences of our lives to leave him in the theatre after he had fallen asleep clutching his teddy bear.

It seemed to take forever but was actually only about 45 minutes before we were taken back down to collect him. I could hear Sam screaming as soon as we came out of the lift and I ran into the recovery room to see Sam staring about him hysterically, looking down at his chest where the Hickman line was. He was crying out, 'Why me, why me?'

We returned to the ward, trying to calm him, and our nurse rushed off to get a sedative for Sam. He drifted off to sleep and David and I wept inconsolably.

When Sam awoke he was quite a different boy. He calmly looked at his Hickman line and asked for some food. It was the first, but would not be the last, time that Sam would bounce back from what seemed a traumatic event, and David and I would be left gaping with astonishment at our son's strength. I believe that the healing Sam received contributed to this inner strength, as I have seen similar things happen many times with patients who are receiving healing.

Our link with the outside world was the parents' phone in the corridor outside our room. We, along with all the other parents, were able to receive calls on it. That afternoon we received a phone call from an old friend of David's, Felicity Evans, who he had known well in his teens.

There is a belief that suggests that there is no such thing as a coincidence; we all meet the people we need to meet at the right time – we just need to be open to realising that fact. Certainly Felicity was a good example of the concept and would turn out to be a great friend and helper over the coming months.

Felicity was a mine of information about the alternative help that we might be interested in. She was very interested in nutrition and had good ideas on what foods might support Sam best at this time. It might have been helpful to follow some of the advice regarding foods, but for the most part – rightly or wrongly – we allowed Sam to eat whatever he fancied. We had been told Sam would lose his appetite and I did not want him to stop eating altogether by suddenly asking him to eat foods that were unknown to him. I believe that we are what we eat, but it was difficult to implement extreme ideas in the hospital setting. I hoped to address the matter of nutrition more easily when I had Sam safely at home. Felicity also suggested that I may want to look into Bach flower remedies, which I had already considered, and offered advice on how to help Sam articulate difficult feelings.

Shortly after David had returned home to collect Nick the nurses arrived with Sam's chemo. It was alarming, to say the least, to see how well protected they were, with gowns and goggles, and it was not a happy thought that this highly toxic drug was being infused into my son. I encouraged Sam to imagine the chemo as one of the characters from his Mortal Combat game, going into battle with the bad cells in his body. He quite liked the idea and we happily passed the time blasting the bad cells until he fell asleep.

That night I wrote away to a radionics practitioner. These practitioners require a sample of hair from the patient through which they claim they can tap into the vibrational frequencies given off from the sample. By placing the hair on a specially designed box, it is said that this box is able to detect imbalances in the body. Upon analysis the practitioner will recommend treatment in the form of herbs or nutritional supplements. This is believed to be a way of tuning into a body's energy patterns and is thought to be very helpful as an additional treatment for many illnesses. I hoped from what I knew of radionics that it might be helpful in alleviating some of the side effects of Sam's treatment. I knew Sam's bone marrow would be attacked and that neutropenia could not be avoided, but I felt if we could help with nausea and any infections that may attack as a complication of not having a healthy immune system it was bound to be beneficial to Sam.

My letter to the practitioner included, as requested, a sample of hair from Sam. As I cut a lock of his hair I cried, wondering how much longer Sam would have his beautiful blond hair. The nurses also injected Sam with anti-sickness drugs to help prevent any nausea he may have. We were told that with the right amount of anti-sickness drugs Sam should not have a problem with nausea. In fact, many of the children did suffer with vomiting and nausea, but Sam was very rarely troubled by it, only having a problem if he had a high temperature. This was obviously very good for Sam's morale and I believe he was helped by the healing and other therapies. I based this observation on seeing that Sam's journey, even this early on, was turning out to be far less of an ordeal for him than for some of his peers. This would become even more obvious as the months passed.

I was still following the simple process of channelling light through me and into Sam. I made a sign for our door saying 'Please do not disturb, healing in progress!' I didn't want to offend anyone but I felt we needed a peaceful uninterrupted time of fifteen minutes or so to give Sam healing. The nurses were excellent at not disturbing us, understanding that for us it was an important part of Sam's care. I often had conversations lasting well into the night with the night staff who were interested in what I was doing when the sign was up and had noticed that Sam was very well for a child with his condition. The doctors and staff were all aware of the other therapies that I was using – I thought this was essential – and I think the general opinion, even from those who may not have believed in it, was that I could do no harm, and I was left alone to do whatever I thought was helpful.

CHAPTER 6

The following morning Sam woke up as bright as a button. My experience with chemo to date had been with Mum's treatment, and she had felt very sick indeed, so this was a great relief.

Sam and I had come to an agreement that if he did not want to see the hospital teacher he would have to agree to let me do some simple maths, spelling and reading with him so that he would not be left behind at school. He agreed to the idea happily. I was, of course, though I didn't know it at the time, making a bit of a rod for my own back as it was always a struggle to get him working. I was after all only 'Mum' and as such he tried to get away with murder!

However, I would have agreed to anything to keep him happy at that time and so mornings became school time, followed by lunch, followed by visitors and endless games of pool in the afternoon and evenings.

The staff were excellent and the chemotherapy was always put up (infused) during the evening to try and give Sam freedom during the day. We had an overabundance of visitors during those first few weeks and cards seemed to arrive from all over the country and indeed the world. David had a lot of contacts abroad and they all sent their best wishes and said they would be praying for Sam. It was very comforting to know that so many people were thinking of Sam and sending positive thoughts.

The Harry Edwards Healing Sanctuary was very supportive. I had contacted them after another mum on the ward had told me that they offered absent healing. All they required was a letter or phone call updating them on Sam's condition every week. In return, each week they responded with a letter offering support and uplift not only for Sam, but for myself.

From the many books I had read when my mother had been ill I knew how important it was to look at the emotional wellbeing of the patient alongside the more obvious physical wellbeing.

Sam had told me that he very much liked being in hospital, as he didn't have to attend school and he had plenty of games and attention! All in all he was not as keen to get well and go home as I would have liked him to be, so I was anxious to address his emotional state.

I had been given details of Peter Clifford, a healer who used Bach flower remedies, by Felicity Evans. Bach flower remedies refer to the products developed by Dr Edward Bach, who worked as a bacteriologist and homeopath in London. He believed that illness was a result of mental or emotional imbalance, and that the unique energetic property of a plant could be used to rectify the imbalance and create wholeness. Using the homeopathic law of potentisation (the theory that tiny amounts of something concentrate its effects) he reasoned that the healing effect of plants might also be contained in the morning dew found on flowers. Dr Bach believed that harmful emotions were the main cause of disease and he classified the various emotions into seven main categories. These were then subdivided into 38 negative feelings, each negative emotion being associated with a different plant.

I contacted Peter. His method of prescribing the correct remedy was to use a sample of Sam's hair, which I had sent him, and apply a technique referred to as 'dowsing' to discover which remedies were going to help Sam most at that time. Peter's reports, which arrived every month, were amazingly accurate.

Flower remedies and essences are liquid preparations and are intended for self-help use. The remedies are sold in concentrated form and you place a few drops on the tongue or dilute them in liquid. Sam took the required few drops of the remedies on his tongue four times a day with no complaint.

Dr Bach also developed a compound of five flowers called rescue remedy to be used in emergency situations or for trauma, and I was able to buy a bottle of this in the local Boots. I used it frequently – apart from anything else it had brandy in it, which caused us great amusement! Peter added his own expertise as a healer to the formulas, which included insights into Sam's emotions that I found very helpful. As one remedy was used up Peter would look at Sam's hair sample again, dowse again and send us a new remedy based on the original hair sample. As time went on I also used flower remedies for myself as I became more and more aware that I had to address my own trauma if I wanted to be strong and positive for Sam.

I also visited the local crystal shop and healing centre in St Albans and they suggested I try healing on Sam every day using a crystal called a peridot. No one seems to know for sure how crystals work, but research in America had shown that this particular crystal had some measurable effect on the acidic surroundings of cancer cells. Rose quartz is good for emotional healing, amethyst for headaches, malachite for stomach problems, lapis for anxiety and jade for the heart.

Practitioners of modern-day crystal therapy believe in the crystals' capacity to store and amplify any power source fed into them. They believe in the stones' ability to work as conductors, allowing them to focus energy via a person's thoughts to stimulate healing, both physical and non-physical. So when I gave Sam healing I would place the crystals on Sam's body and then heal in the normal way; in this way I hoped to intensify the effect I may be having in healing Sam.

Sam was very co-operative with all of these alternative therapies; at the beginning he accused me of being 'potty' but as time went on he became more and more interested in some of the therapies we were using. Healing was always his favourite as he didn't have to do anything except lie there while I got on with it and he said that it made him feel warm and relaxed.

Although I was able to give healing to Sam, I had not attended any official courses – what knowledge I did have, I had picked up from books when Mum was ill – and I wanted to make sure Sam wasn't missing out on anything a more experienced healer might have to offer. This worried me, but when I wrote to Betty Shine (a well-known healer and medium now in spirit) she told me not to be so silly: 'Mothers are the best healers.' I was introduced to Betty Shine by another mother on the ward, who gave me one of Betty's books to read. In the book I read that Betty also offered absent healing and I contacted her to ask for help. She agreed to add Sam's name to the list of people that she was sending absent healing to, and while relieved at what she had said about my healing, I still felt drawn to look for some more experienced healers.

I contacted a healer who I had read an article about who seemed to have a good reputation. He sent me a diagram explaining colour healing and a brief description of what to do and the colours he prescribed – this was an unusual way of healing that I had not read about before. The instructions were that I needed two people for the procedure, one on each side of Sam, and we then had to visualise the colours prescribed for Sam into his body. To enable me to do this I enlisted David's help and together we tried to heal Sam. Previously I had been giving Sam healing at night when there were few people around, but as we were trying this new regime I had to catch David when he came to visit in the early evening. It must have caused a few raised eyebrows on the ward as the sign I had made for the door went up more and more frequently. David did his best with this colour healing, but he was uncomfortable with the process and I soon reverted to working by myself.

The days passed quite quickly, falling into a routine of late breakfast – schoolwork – lunch – play until David and Nick arrived for their visit in the evening. Nick seemed to be coping well with all the changes. He told me later that while he was at school he didn't really think about the situation and was able to just get on with life. Only when he came up to the hospital did he have to face what was happening. In my work with other families since Sam's passing I have found this to be a very common pattern of behaviour from siblings of the child who is ill. It is no good expecting a teenage boy to explore his feelings and discuss them with anyone if he has no desire to do so. David was back at work – we still had bills to pay, as did all the other families on the ward. Inevitably this meant that the fathers had less involvement with the protocols and day-to-day developments on the ward, but we all just got on with it.

Sam was tolerating the chemo extremely well; anti-sickness drugs were given in advance of any anticipated problems, but even so the staff were beginning to notice that Sam was coping really well, and some nurses began to wonder about why this might be and to take an interest in what other therapies we were using. Some of the nurses listened with great interest when I told them about the methods we were using, saying that they were interested in finding out more for themselves, but others were clearly not interested and avoided any talk of alternative therapies. That was fine with me, since I didn't feel as though I needed to prove anything either way – the proof for me was that Sam was coping well with his treatment.

The treatment protocol suggests that once you are neutropenic it is usual to develop an infection. Patients will feel very ill and will need to receive a course of antibiotics. With antibiotics to support you, it is hoped that you will recover and can then be allowed home for a short break between treatments.

It is usual to see a problem within seven days of finishing the chemotherapy, but Sam did not respond 'normally' and remained well for almost 21 days.

We were about to be allowed home for the week, however, when Sam suddenly developed a very high temperature. Even then, though, no infection could be found in his blood tests. After a week of antibiotics we were finally allowed home.

During the time we had been waiting for Sam's marrow to recover, we had another interview with our consultant to discuss the results of the chromosome tests they had been running from the original bone marrow aspirate test.

I had seen a number of parents being summoned to the parent interview room since we had been in Great Ormond Street and I knew that it inevitably meant bad news. Knowing this, I thought I was mentally prepared for what our consultant was about to tell us – I was wrong.

We were told that Sam had the AML associated with the worst

prognosis, with a success rate of only 25 per cent. Even though I had been half-expecting bad news, it was still enough of a shock to make my body break out in a sweat and start to shake. I could not look at David or I would have broken down, so we asked a few more questions and then went back to our room.

Sam looked anxiously at our faces when we returned and I gave him a hug and said that all was well. Inside I was an emotional wreck and I could not stop my hands from shaking. I escaped into the kitchen to make a coffee. Harry's mum Jane was there; she took one look at me and asked what the matter was. When I managed to tell her, Jane was very reassuring and told me that on their previous stay Harry had been the opposite – he had been in the most hopeful group of statistics and now here they were again with the leukaemia back. She had also known several children on the ward, with apparently no hope on paper, pull through. It was just what I wanted to hear and what I needed to hear. At that moment I resolved not to think of the prognosis but just to focus on getting Sam well and living each day to the full.

The following day was when we were allowed home for the week, while we waited for Sam's blood count to rise sufficiently to test the bone marrow. It takes time for the marrow to recover following chemotherapy before an aspirate test (to look inside the marrow) that is necessary to establish if the chemotherapy had put Sam in remission. If this test is done too soon it can show a false positive result.

It was wonderful to be home. However, I had lots to do – it was my opportunity to arrange some experienced hands-on healing, which I desperately wanted Sam to have.

CHAPTER 7

It was the first time that we had been together as a family for eight weeks. We all slotted back into normal family life as if nothing had happened but, of course, our whole world had been turned upside down.

I had been put in touch with Claudine, a healer who lived in a nearby village, and she very kindly rearranged her schedule to be able to visit Sam while he was at home. As Claudine entered our house I was overwhelmed with the feelings of loving warmth and kindness that she brought with her. She chatted quietly with us for a while and explained to Sam what she would be doing. She explained that she would ask him to sit quietly in a chair while she stood behind him and laid her hands on his head. She explained to him that energy would flow through her and into him and that he may feel rather warm during the process.

Sam was behaving like a naughty little boy, running around the room in high spirits while Claudine talked, but he soon quietened under her hands and relaxed for the ten minutes or so that it took her to complete her healing.

While Claudine was healing, I sat quietly in the same room and became very aware of the energy she was creating. My toes and fingers started to tingle and I felt very emotional. I was somehow linking in with Claudine's healing. She explained this was often the case if people had some psychic ability themselves. She said that I no doubt would be able to help Sam by continuing with the healing sessions in the hospital.

We talked for some time after Sam had run off to play and I felt very uplifted by the time she left. I was very reassured, as I had witnessed a healing from an experienced practitioner that was no different from what I had been practising for the past two months.

During the time we were at home we packed as many treats and outings in as we could. Sam had boundless energy and wanted to be out enjoying himself. This was also a good example of how healing can help people. So often people who are having cancer treatments look completely washed out with no energy to enjoy themselves. This was just not true for Sam – he was very well indeed. I insisted Sam eat as many hot meals as he would tolerate to make up for all the burgers over the past month; roast dinners with lots of fresh vegetables were a favourite on the menu during that week at home.

A community nurse called at home to check Sam's blood count by taking blood from his line, but apart from a transfusion of blood products (platelets), which we obtained from our local hospital, we pretty much managed to steer clear of medical people for that week. It was wonderful. All too soon, however, the time came when we had to return to Great Ormond Street for a bone-marrow test. Sam would then be starting his second course of chemotherapy.

The nurses greeted us cheerfully and settled us back into our room. Because we had only been away a week we had been able to leave our cards and some personal belongings in the room; it was like returning to our second home.

At the time for his bone-marrow aspirate Sam went nervously into the treatment room, reluctantly holding out his line for the ketamine to be injected. I was sent into the adjoining room as soon as Sam appeared to be asleep and I was just settling down to wait when I heard the most horrific scream. It was like nothing I have ever heard before, and it tore at my heart. There was another mum waiting in the room with me and her eyes mirrored my horror. I knew it was Sam and when the second scream came I launched myself back into the treatment room like a lioness in full flight. Sam was moving around on the bed and it was quite obvious that he had not received enough of the drug – he was looking around the room with fear in his eyes. The staff said it would be all right, that he would not remember anything about it, and were quickly topping up his line with more ketamine. I stayed in the room holding Sam's head and talking calmly to him as he went out for the count again. I stayed with him while they completed the procedure, but I will never forget that look on his face as he screamed at the sensation of the needle going into his hipbone from where the sample is taken.

I carried him from the treatment room, laying him down on the recovery bed, and tried to stay calm for his sake. I knew he would be awake soon and I didn't want to upset him by showing him my distress. The doctors were wrong, however. Sam *did* remember the feelings in the room that day and each subsequent test was a complete nightmare. We had to hold him down forcibly to administer the drug.

Sam started his second chemo that night. The test had revealed that he was not in remission but the blast cells had been reduced from 85 per cent to 45 per cent – it was a start. It was nowhere near the hoped-for figure of 5 per cent that would mean Sam was in remission, but at least it showed the chemo was having some effect. We knew the routine by now and Sam slept a great deal of the time, which was a blessing, but when he was awake he felt very well. We continued using all the therapies that had been set up for the initial round of chemo – absent healing, flower remedies, homeopathic remedies – and, of course, I continued giving healing every night.

It was about this time that the battles over food began. Sam had heard from various members of staff that if you didn't feel like eating that was OK, because you could have a food supplement given through the line. This was totally unacceptable to me. I had it fixed in my mind that the will to eat was closely linked to the will to live. I became an expert at turning out home cooking from the parents' kitchen and feel sure that I could cook a roast dinner on a camp stove now if I had to! I also kept a large supply of goodies in our room for when Nick visited; there were always home-made fairy cakes, dried fruit and chocolate available, and Sam happily snacked constantly. All the foods that were normally restricted he could now have as much as he liked and to my delight he continued to eat. All ideas of nutrition went out of the window as I fought to keep Sam eating normally instead of through a tube. It was a battle, but one I was very glad to have fought and won.

Sam continued to feel and look very well despite often having a temperature of 40 degrees. His reaction to the chemo seemed to be forming a pattern. Very high temperatures meant he had to be put on antibiotics as a preventative measure in case he really did have an infection. His temperature would go down when his marrow and blood counts recovered, regardless of which antibiotic was used. Sam was quite unlike the other children in that no infection ever showed on the cultures that were taken.

It was during this second course of treatment that Sam began to lose his hair. Even though we had prepared for it by buying loads of trendy hats, it was still a major blow to Sam and he cried bitterly over it. When his best friend Tom who lived close to us at home visited, Sam would always wear a hat and was very worried that Tom would not like him without hair. Tom (also aged seven) was a magnificent friend to Sam, visiting regularly. Like most children, who did not take a scrap of notice of Sam's appearance, Tom was more interested in what new game Sam had or whether I had made another batch of fairy cakes for our room! Sam soon relaxed in his company and within weeks was not bothering to wear the hats unless he went outside the ward. We were very fortunate to have been allowed to keep the same room for this second course of treatment. We had certainly put our stamp on it and it was very much 'our room'. Cards covered the walls and hats hung on every available surface – Fanny the electronic pump was especially useful as a hat stand.

In the course of trying a number of alternative therapies, I had built up quite a large collection of crystals in the room. I had read about crystals and the various healing properties they were meant to carry. We had rose quartz for love, a blood stone (green in colour) that was meant to help cleanse the spleen, and various others that Sam had liked the look of. I put these crystals under Sam's pillow at night. It's a wonder he could sleep at all given all the rocks he was sleeping on! I often see crystals in the rooms of patients at

University College Hospital where I work now and am happy that it is so much more accepted that patients are using these beautiful stones to help themselves. We joked with the staff that the room was my crystal cave and that I practised weird and wonderful ceremonies in there, and certainly the consultant sometimes seemed a little uneasy when he came to see us on his weekly rounds!

We also brought Sam's duvet with his 'Pamela Anderson' quilt cover to brighten the whole room up. She caused quite a stir when the doctors were doing their rounds but Sam had always been a great admirer of *Bay Watch*, and liked to have his duvet from home.

It was while we were waiting for Sam's counts to recover after the second course of chemotherapy that we had the opportunity to get to know the staff a little better. As with normal life outside the hospital, there are people you immediately bond with who you really feel care about their work, and there are those who give you the impression they are just doing their job, but on Robin Ward, without exception, the nursing staff were excellent in their craft. One such was Anita; she took Sam under her wing and brought him a little china teddy bear for him to tell his very private thoughts and worries to. He took to the idea very well and we had sessions late into the night where he would talk to the bear and I would be allowed to listen. Sometimes an answer was required from the bear (who Sam had named Alex) and I would be allowed to answer for Alex. These sessions we called 'Alex-time'. Since Sam was able to tell Alex things that he obviously felt would worry me too much it was a wonderful way to communicate and this way I was still able to know what was going through Sam's mind.

It was while having one of these talks that I became really concerned that Sam was quite happy to stay at hospital (in his words, for 'a very long time') rather than have to go back to school and begin to live in the real world again. I looked for ways to motivate him to get better, but without success. I had thought that if we could get inside his mind by the use of a child hypnotherapist we could plant the right seeds and I contacted a specialist with that in mind. I did talk at length to her about Sam and my concerns regarding his negative feelings about school and life in general, and she was able to offer me and him very useful advice on how to stimulate positive thoughts. Sam was not hypnotised – this was one thing he would not co-operate with – but the therapist gave me good ideas on how to help Sam on a daily basis, such as talking as if we were already in the future and Sam was completely well again. See ourselves on holiday as a family enjoying ourselves, see Sam playing with a small dog that he had always wanted to own. She advised me not to ask him to visualise himself at school; we could afford to work on that particular block when we had got Sam well and at home again. All this seemed to be enough for him to relax about the future as the therapist and myself assured him that he need not go to school until he was ready, and he could have a home tutor if required. All of this really helped and Sam compiled a list of all the things he wanted to do when we left hospital.

Some of the nurses were also worried about Sam's state of mind at that point for another reason. He had been found acting out the role of choking and dying, which they thought was very worrying. On the other hand, I thought this was very normal for a child undergoing the things and confronting the sort of issues he was having to. I felt that Sam was handling things very well and didn't need yet more people questioning him, so when there were a few mutterings of 'child psychologist needed', I very quickly squashed them. The nurses are wonderful in offering support on every level, but I believe that sometimes families can help themselves without professional involvement of this kind. I accept that for some families this kind of help is invaluable but, depending on the child, it can be more disturbing to be asked to talk to a stranger than to leave the family to resolve problems of this nature in their own way. Sam was at this point still quite selective about who he opened up to and I didn't see how a child psychologist could be of much help to him. The phase of Sam acting dead eventually passed and it was never mentioned again, not even in our Alex-time.

During this stay in hospital I had been taught how to take care of Sam's Hickman line, how to change the dressing and how to take blood for the regular blood tests he would be needing. Sam preferred me to take care of things as much as possible and I was happy to learn. It was a bit nerve-racking initially, as you are potentially leaving your child open to infection if you do not practise the sterile technique correctly, but it was very much worth the effort as we didn't have to wait for a community nurse to call any more, which made us more independent.

In between Sam's school lessons with me and my lessons learning to take care of the Hickman line, we played a lot of pool in the ward's reception area. It was while we were playing there late one afternoon that the door flew open and James burst into our life.

CHAPTER 8

James was a lovely boy who looked full of mischief and was obviously quite at home on the ward. Unfortunately for James and his family he had been treated for AML once before and he had subsequently relapsed. I was very pleased to see someone of Sam's age appear on the ward as – apart from Harry, who was going through such a tough time that we didn't see much of him – most of the other patients were babies at that time. However, I was horrified that this was yet another relapsed AML back on the ward. James's parents were naturally in a great state of shock and were not holding back on their feelings. Sam looked at me and I knew immediately that he was thinking 'Why are they all relapsing when Mum is telling me that I am going to get better?' I took Sam back to our room and prepared myself for the questions that I knew Sam would be asking. Sam immediately voiced his concern about children coming back for treatment and I answered truthfully that all AML cases were different, and some of them needed a little bit more treatment after they had finished the first time. I reassured Sam that he did not have the same type of leukaemia as Harry and James, so it would be different for him. He was happy with the explanation and let the subject drop. Conveniently for me we could hear a lot of excitement in the corridor outside our room and off he went to investigate.

Harry had his bone marrow tested that day and his parents had just been told that he was in remission! The whole ward was delighted and his parents were understandably ecstatic. This meant that they could now go ahead and have a bone-marrow transplant with Harry's sister as the donor. It was FLAG that had been successful in obtaining a remission for Harry and I resolved to find out more about it just in case we were not successful with the conventional treatments. Harry's parents had already advised me that I should make myself aware of what was available, as the consultants were not very forthcoming about other treatments that could be attempted once the normal routes had failed. I hoped that we would not need to look further afield but a little voice inside me kept nudging me to know as much as I could.

Harry and his family left that day for a week's break before returning for their transplant. The whole ward was very uplifted by the news that Harry was in remission. The ward was like a big family. Everyone rejoiced when things were going well and we all grieved together when the news for one or the other of us was not so good. All around us children were obtaining their longed-for remission but although Sam looked very well, he wasn't in remission. We would have to wait until his marrow recovered from his latest treatment and then undergo another aspirate test, before we would know if Sam had achieved it yet.

It was around this time that I was given a book about how positive thinking and affirmations can help us beat illnesses back. It was a great book to read as without it I may have found it hard to keep so focused and positive. It taught me to look inside myself and heal emotions that I was struggling with. Most of all, it taught me the value of performing positive affirmations at times of stress and doubt. Before I went to sleep at night and the first thing I did when I woke in the morning was to repeat to myself, 'I release all fears and doubts, Sam is well.' Whenever things got on top of me I would go into the bathroom, look in the mirror and repeat the affirmation. Sam, of course, thought I was completely potty but it kept me sane and the message was going into my subconscious.

We had been given the name of a healer who was willing to come to the hospital to give Sam hands-on healing. The healer came to see us twice during our stay in hospital, once during one of Sam's spectacular high temperatures. As seems to be the case with all healers, he had a great presence about him and created a very calm atmosphere as soon as he entered our room. He brought with him a soft teddy holding an 'S' in its arms, which Sam took to straightaway. It was a very short session but Sam seemed a little calmer after the healing. Again the healer did nothing different to what I was practising every night on Sam, but I was reassured by the knowledge that Sam was getting the very best of help.

Sam had become more outgoing as the weeks wore on and he was to be seen running up and down the ward with his syringe water pistol, soaking doctors and nurses indiscriminately. This is not to say that he did not have bad days but on the whole he tolerated the chemo with relative ease. We knew that the next course of chemo we were scheduled to have had a bad reputation for destroying the stomach lining and could possibly cause him some problems, but for the moment he was doing very well indeed. Sam was enjoying a quality of life that many of his peers were not. He was now very comfortable that I gave him healing every day, no longer calling me 'potty' and happy to talk to the nurses about the alternative remedies he was taking and happily showing off his collection of crystals.

We also met a very important person at around this time. Bettina was a volunteer on the ward. She came in for a few days during the week and played with Sam when he felt up to it and became a friend to us both. She had become a volunteer after the child of a friend had become seriously ill and had been treated at the hospital; she was another invaluable source of information. Her friend had also used a lot of alternative remedies, one of them involving having her house cleansed by dowsers. Apparently these people could identify any environmental stress within the home that may suppress some people's immune systems. Environmental stress includes natural distorted electromagnetic fields that emanate under pressure from the earth (goethic stress), resonances of toxic materials (such as glues, varnish, lead paints) and the use and abuse of the electromagnetic spectrum including electric appliances, radio broadcasting and associated installations. If a home does have environmental stress dowsers believe that a person might find it more difficult to recover from cancer or any illness because the body would be battling against the electromagnetic bombardments rather than using all their energy to recover from illness.

The idea really appealed to me in addition to the other alternative therapies we were trying, I felt it was important to make the house as safe a place as possible for Sam's eventual homecoming. I contacted Jacqui Beacon (a dowser and kinesiologist) and as we spoke on the telephone she described Sam to me in great detail (fascinating, as she had never met Sam or anyone else connected to our family). We arranged for Jacqui and her partner to visit our house when I was at home that Friday.

Before Harry's mum had left for their week away she handed me lots of paperwork that she had collected from different sources: addresses of healers, various remedies and self-help groups. One of the things to catch my eye was a herbal remedy called Essiac. It was a North American remedy and it could be obtained via a network in the UK. I rang one of the contact numbers and spoke to a lady called Doris. She had been very ill with cancer for many years and the doctors had told her she should be dead by now; however, she was still going strong and she believed that it was entirely due to Essiac. Doris said she would send me some of the herbs with instructions as to how to make up the solution, and the instructions for dosage.

I knew from what Doris had said regarding the taste of Essiac that I would have a devil of a job to get Sam to agree to take the remedy, but I felt it was one more thing to have up my sleeve if we needed it.

There was sometimes a cost involved in the therapies I used during Sam's illness, though very often there was no charge initially from the people that I contacted, merely an overwhelming desire to help Sam. As time went on cost did sometimes become an issue and I was aware for some families it might have been even more so. Having seen how much good I felt these therapies were doing for Sam I eventually came to the strong conviction that something had to change. Patients should be able to access help from healing without having to worry about the cost, especially if they are an in-patient in a hospital – they have enough to think about without having to worry about paying for healing when they need it most. As time went on this conviction grew, until a few years later I finally felt I had to do something about it.

CHAPTER 9

We had fallen into a routine of me returning home every Friday evening to have a night at home with Nick, while David stayed at the hospital with Sam. I had arranged for the dowsers to come that Friday evening and I was very excited that this might be another important piece of the jigsaw puzzle to get Sam well and, more importantly, to help him stay well.

I did not know what to expect and so when Jacqui and her partner Dave arrived, I was relieved to see they were very normal-looking folk! We had a short chat about their work and they explained how electromagnetic stress could affect the health of the people living in the house. I must admit that at that time a lot of what they told me went completely over my head, partly because I was only concerned with doing whatever would help Sam, and partly because this was my one evening at home and I wanted to make sure I had some quality time with Nick. First of all Jacqui and Dave did a space-clearing process where they cleared the adverse emotions that lodge in the fabric of a building and adversely affect its occupants. Then they considered family members to see how their energies were interfacing with the atmosphere of the property. Using kinesiology (the study of the mechanics and anatomy of human muscles) they cleared emotional and mental blocks that were affecting my family. Then Dave went through the house, room by room, with a meter measuring the amount of electromagnetic and microwave frequencies being put out by the various pieces of electrical equipment. Jacqui then passed through each room with her dowsing rods to check areas of geopathic stress, which is when the surrounding electrical and natural radiation in an area has an adverse effect on the environment; this may, in turn, have a negative effect on the immune system. Unbeknown to me, they had already spent some time outside the house and in the surrounding area to establish where the nearest electric substation was and various other risk factors. Based on that information, Dave dug two holes in the garden and buried a glass bottle of crystals in each; these were to prevent any negative energies from entering the house. Once this work has been carried out the property remains harmonised for many years. Of course, if any important changes occur in the surrounding environment, such as the erecting of a telephone mast or other major electrical changes, you may need to reconsider your situation.

Meanwhile Jacqui had been checking out where to site the two Energy Mixing Beacons that she had created (glass bottles containing minerals, crystals and a self-cleansing mechanism) by dowsing repeatedly until she was satisfied she had them placed correctly. The products act as an anchor for the harmonisation process.

During the time they had been working, we had been talking about Sam and his illness and my belief that we had been put together in this lifetime to enable us both to overcome the illness he was suffering. Jacqui agreed totally and went on to say that Sam and I had already experienced two previous lifetimes together and that was why the bond was so strong between us. I hadn't any knowledge of previous lifetimes but I found the thought very interesting. (Months later I underwent a past-life regression from an experienced therapist and despite my scepticism found the experience fascinating, although I'm not sure it was particularly useful in helping Sam get well.)

Jacqui taught me how to balance my body to enable me to dowse to establish if the house was clear, so that I could keep it as clear as possible in the future. When I stood up to do as she asked I was nervous that I would not be able to do it. I had to stand perfectly still with my arms to my side and take a few deep breaths to steady myself. Then, with my left hand placed over my stomach and my right hand and arm hanging down straight to my side I was to ask a series of questions out loud to my house to ask whether each room was 'clear' of negative energy. It sounds wacky and it felt wacky but much to my amazement my body would sway very strongly forward for a 'Yes' and backwards for a 'No'. To my delight I was able to dowse straight away and she asked me to check each room by this method one by one to ascertain that all was well.

All was clear until we reached the conservatory and then when I dowsed the answer was no – the room was not clear. Dave and Jacqui went back into the room and dowsed again only to establish that it was not the room that was the problem, but an obelisk that we had brought back from Egypt the previous year. Dave cleansed the offending article and when I dowsed again the room was indeed clear. I was very worried that all the other items that we had brought back from trips abroad could be holding bad vibes on them, but they reassured me that the dowsing would have shown them up if there had been a problem.

The whole procedure took about four hours and when they left I was so elated by what I had witnessed and learned that night that I found it impossible to sleep and was awake for most of the night. Jackie had said that the house might feel a little odd for a few weeks while it settled and indeed it did. If I sat quietly it was as though the house was wrapped in cotton wool and the normal sounds of the house were muffled and quieter than usual. I was very glad we had gone ahead and had the house dowsed as I felt anything that could possibly help Sam, which was within my power to do, should be done. It was an expensive thing to have carried out – it depends on the size of the house and the amount of work carried out – but we had received a lump sum from an insurance policy that week and David and I felt that a few hundred pounds of it was being to put to good use if we used it in this way. I believe it was a great help in making Sam's time at home the best it could be. I felt very uplifted by the day's events and couldn't wait to tell David and Sam all about the dowsers the following day and compare notes with Jane, who had also had her house dowsed. I found the whole experience so inspiring that I have also had the two houses I have lived in since dowsed.

There has been a lot of interest to date in the role of environmental hazards and their possible effect on the amount of childhood cancers and it made complete sense to me to address the matter. I personally feel that where there is a genetic weakness, the added effects of environmental problems can be enough to suppress the immune system and let the cancer develop. I think in time to come we will all know this to be a fact but for the moment it is still a matter for debate.

I believe it's very important, no matter what problem you face, to be as proactive as you can and to help yourself as much as possible. The intention has to be that you are not going to just let things happen to you – you will retain some sense of control. Though a lot of doctors will find you 'difficult' because you may challenge decisions you do not agree with, I believe this will make you as patients or parents 'Exceptional Patients'. If being labelled 'difficult' meant that ultimately Sam would do well, I was happy to be 'difficult'.

I had asked my consultant for up-to-date information on AML and he had very kindly lent me a few books that he himself had written. When he gave me his books, I handed over one of mine by the American oncologist Bernie S. Siegel. I felt we were not communicating as well as we could and hoped the book would help him understand my optimism and positive stance. He accepted the book with a bewildered look and said he would try and find time to read it. When I read Sam's medical notes and letters, however, I saw he had written a letter to another consultant expressing his surprise that I would not accept Sam's prognosis as being fairly hopeless. This prognosis was based on the fact that Sam had been unable to achieve remission at that point. I strongly believe that in the face of uncertainty, there is nothing wrong with hope. Personally I was finding my hope not only in positive thinking and daily affirmations, but also in the continual use of alternative therapies and remedies and especially our daily healing sessions. If only more medical people believed that – along with the vital information that, of course, the doctors must give the patient – no patient should ever be robbed of hope. Perhaps then more patients could be sustained and uplifted and ultimately have a more positive journey with their cancer.

CHAPTER 10

Things at the hospital had once again settled down for the long wait for Sam's counts to rise. I know in my heart that the healing Sam was receiving, from so many different sources, was helping him enormously. Any discomfort Sam experienced seemed light compared to what the other children were suffering. Occasionally he would develop a mouth ulcer and I would immediately contact the radionics practitioner, who would swiftly place a sample of Sam's hair on the 'box' and would then be able to either send a supplement or give me advice on any food I could give Sam that would help him to recover from whatever problem or side effect he was suffering from. Often, as if by magic, the ulcer would disappear the next day. The nurses were sure this was due to Sam's excellent mouth care (he rinsed his mouth with a special solution), and this probably was partly the reason, but I believe the radionics also played a very important role in keeping the side effects to a minimum.

While we were waiting for the counts to rise we were told that our immediate family would be given a simple blood test to establish whether our marrows were compatible with Sam's (this is termed 'tissue typing'). The match has to be as perfect as possible to minimise the risk of rejection, so if Sam needed a transplant it would (apparently) only be possible if the marrow came from one of us, his immediate family. We were told there was a one-in-four chance of one of us being a match for Sam, but we would have to wait several weeks after the blood test for the results. Nick hoped to be the one who was a match for Sam so that he could help. Even though Nick did not find giving blood an easy thing to do – and it took a great deal of courage for him to do so (I know some medical staff feel families put undue pressure on siblings to donate marrow) – when I asked Nick how he felt about being a potential donor he looked at me as if I was mad and said, 'Of course I will, he's my brother.'

By this time I had read so much about AML, and especially Sam's subtype, that I felt very strongly that if at all possible I wanted a transplant to be part of Sam's treatment. This was because his particular leukaemia was well documented as being difficult to get into remission. My reasoning was that if we could achieve a remission once, we needed to do something to keep him in remission. I did not want to risk a relapse and not be able to achieve remission again. It was all very well for me to make this decision but we would still need a match to be able to attempt a transplant and we wouldn't know if one of us was suitable for some time to come. However my intuition, which I was beginning to trust more and more, made me feel sure one of us would be a match for Sam.

Our visitors had by now been reduced to the old faithfuls. We had been in hospital for three months already and people had to get on with their lives. Tom and his family came regularly, as did some of my good friends. Sam's godfather, his beloved 'Uncle Nick', was a very welcome visitor and cheered Sam up when he felt low. Uncle Nick was in the air force and donated an old uniform cap, which looked very dashing, to Sam's collection. Since none of the other children had this unique piece of head wear it made Sam feel pretty special.

Some of our relatives and friends found it hard to believe that Sam was not 'fixed' by now and could not understand the complexities of the treatment and the fact that it was all taking so long. I didn't care how long the treatments took as long as we achieved a healthy boy at the end of it all.

For me the months were flying past and we were now well into December. The third treatment was scheduled to start the week before Christmas and because of this David and I decided to bring our family Christmas forward by a week so we could celebrate it at home. The boys were delighted by this idea (presents a whole week early was a real treat), and so I began to go out and buy gifts in Oxford Street, which was nearby. Going out into the mayhem of London at Christmas is strange enough at most times, but for me it was a culture shock after the ward. I must have been a strange sight wandering around the shops, my arms filled with presents, tears streaming down my face. I found the Christmas lights, happy faces and Christmas carols very hard to take when our own life and many others on the ward were so intense and painful.

Christmas is for children, and for my child and others like him it was going to be a miserable time fighting for his – and their – health. The nurses and other staff on the ward were doing their best to decorate and create a happy environment and by the time we left for our break the ward looked very seasonal. We had told the boys that we were lucky – not only were we having an early Christmas at home, when we arrived back on the ward we would be having another Christmas with, no doubt, lots of other presents! It's amazing how positive thinking helps and they seemed more than happy with our plans. The long-awaited day arrived; Sam's counts had risen enough for us to be allowed home. One of the first things we did was to go out and buy the biggest Christmas tree we could find. This had become a bit of a tradition in the Buxton house and this year was not going to be any different. We allocated a day to be Christmas Day and set about with our preparations. However, among all the Christmas preparations, we didn't forget to continue Sam's healing. I was able to arrange some more healing from Claudine, who always dropped everything to come and see Sam on his rare trips home. We had also been introduced by Felicity to another healer called Kim, who had his own chapel in his back garden. It was a wonderful little place, with its own very special atmosphere. Kim was a delight to meet and Sam seemed very comfortable there – he complained it smelled a bit funny as Kim liked to use incense, but the healing was very similar to the way I did it and so he was happy enough. The ever-approaching marrow test and the desperate need for one of us to be a match for Sam were beginning to take their toll on us. When Kim suggested healing would be of benefit to me, I eagerly took up the suggestion. As I received healing from Kim in his sanctuary at the bottom of the garden I felt for the first time what Sam had been receiving. A warm glow filled every part of my body and a feeling of peace pushed away the fear that was ever present in my life. I had got so used to my heart feeling like a rock that when the healing eased some of the stress I felt lighter and happier than I had since the day Sam had been diagnosed. I resolved to access healing for myself whenever I could from then on. It helped me in so many ways; importantly, I felt more positive inside myself, so I wasn't just saying positive things, I was now feeling them as well. I have continued to receive healing since that first experience as I believe that if healing is used regularly it can have a positive prophylactic effect. This changes the experience from being reactive to preventative.

In my work now I always encourage the relatives of my patients within the hospital to receive healing as well. I know if I'm helping the parent/spouse/friend I am also helping the patient. Who we are with and their attitudes to our illness is very important in our journey through cancer, as well as helping the 'helpers' to get through the situation themselves.

We had a wonderful pretend Christmas Day. The boys wanted for nothing and we celebrated in fine style. It was very strange to go into the shops the following day and hear people talking about all the things they still needed to do. Our Christmas was over and done with and now we had to begin to prepare ourselves for the next course of treatment and the dreaded marrow test.

CHAPTER 11

The ward was decorated to help us all feel more seasonal and the staff were going to be cooking Christmas lunch for all the patients and parents. First, though, we had to have the marrow test to ascertain if Sam was in remission. Sam had to be forcibly held down to administer the drug but the end result was well worth the wait and terror. Sam's leukaemia cells were now down to 10%!

It was the best news we had received in a long time and although Sam was still not in remission (remission being classed as a figure under 5 per cent) we all hoped that the next course of chemotherapy would put that right. To put things in perspective on how severe Sam's leukaemia was, most of the other children had obtained their remission after the first course of chemotherapy and their ongoing treatment was to consolidate that remission. For us, however, even after two courses of chemotherapy, it was our first taste of being close to remission and it felt wonderful. We still had a very long way to go, though.

Sam started his third course of chemo straight away and the effects were almost immediately felt. He suffered terrible stomach problems and we were both awake all night as I helped poor little Sam to the bathroom to cope with the uncontrollable diarrhoea. He lost a great deal of weight and for the first time since we had been diagnosed he looked a very sick boy indeed.

It was also the only time since treatment had begun that he needed to be fed through his Hickman line and that was a major blow to us.

This was our first taste of what some of the other children had been going through; I liked to think it was because we'd been using all the therapies and healing before. Although it didn't seem that all the therapies I could give him were helping on this occasion, I didn't give up on finding as much alternative help for Sam as I could.

It was about this time in my depths of despair that I wrote away to a guru in Germany called Mother Meera. One of the healers had given me her address, telling me that I would not get a reply but that I would notice a change for the better if I wrote. I wrote away in good faith and desperation – and was rewarded a few days later by Sam suddenly sitting up in his bed, saying he had been sick long enough and that he wanted to get up and have something to eat! It really was a remarkable change and Sam recovered very quickly from that point. Some of the staff were very surprised at Sam's complete turnaround – he was not reacting in the usual way – but they had got used to Sam dealing with things differently to the other children on the ward. They seemed to be just happy for us that he was on the mend and they and we could once again have the benefit of his cheerful nature and beaming smile.

Christmas Day came and went and we had a few family visitors and the lunch that the nurses had so kindly prepared. Everyone tried their best to make it a happy day and the standard of acting from parents and, probably, children should have won us all Oscars! I think we all breathed a sigh of relief when it was over and we could concentrate on the treatment again.

New Year's Eve was similar with the parents trying to keep jolly and talking hopefully with a 'New Year, New Start' mentality. Sam was very pleased with himself as he managed to throw up exactly on the stroke of midnight!

The New Year for us started in miraculous fashion. Nick was indeed a match for Sam, which meant that a transplant could be planned if Sam's leukaemia would just go into remission. The nursing staff seemed genuinely delighted for us, and our spirits rose in leaps and bounds. Sam continued to feel better and began to eat normally again; I continued to give him regular healing, even though my faith had been shaken by Sam's decline this time. Healing had helped all the other times and I reasoned that this time had just been unfortunate. And anyway, I believed that Mother Meera had more than a little to do with Sam's recovery.

The days passed fairly quickly as James's mum had become a firm friend by now – we enjoyed putting the world to rights with a glass of wine most evenings, while the boys raced around the wards with their loaded 50ml syringes causing havoc. David and I even managed to go out for a drink one evening, the first time we had done that in over four months! I found that sort of reality very difficult to cope with and always came back to the ward with a kind of 'who am I kidding?' feeling.

We had to wait for Sam's counts to recover once more before we could have a few days at home, and then we would be able to look at Sam's marrow to see what effect the terrible chemo had had on the leukaemia. We left the hospital with a lighter heart than we had for some considerable time, and felt like a proper family for the first time in ages during our time at home.

Sam was in need of a large carrot dangling in front of him, giving him something to aim for. One of David's aunts had by chance sent Sam a card with Jack Russell puppies on the front and so the idea had been born – Sam was to have a puppy! He was entranced with the idea and the promise was made: as soon as he was well he would have a puppy.

Once the bone-marrow test had been performed, we were ushered into our consultant's office to hear the results. The news was not good. The last course of treatment had had little to no effect and Sam's leukaemia still stood at 10 per cent. Our consultant left us with the impression that anything we might do now had little chance of success. It was a major blow and David and I were shattered once again. We asked the consultant about the treatment that Harry had been given called FLAG and he looked surprised that we even knew about it. I asked whether it was worth trying on Sam and he replied that it was possible. He thought we could go ahead and try it if that was what we wanted. Harry had been the first child on the unit to undergo FLAG and it had achieved remission for him even though he had resistant disease. I sent out a silent thank you to Harry for making it possible to follow in his footsteps. To be able to know there was more treatment to be had (if you just knew what to ask for) was a definite advantage.

We left the hospital that day with our hearts in our boots. I could not conceal my distress from Sam and we all cried together for a while and then Sam rallied us all around by pointing out that Harry had done very well on FLAG and was now having a transplant and so we weren't to worry, FLAG would do the trick!

When we arrived back at Great Ormond Street the following Monday we were all feeling much more optimistic. The new chemo was given every night and due to the fact that part of the regime was a 'growth factor' (growth factors help the marrow to recover more quickly), Sam's counts remained high, which meant that we were free to wander around London during the day. I continued with my healing regime and Sam tolerated the treatment very well – for longer than other children on the protocol; we were allowed home every day after the chemo had ended. This continued until his counts dropped and he was once again neutropenic and open to infection, when we were confined to the ward again.

During the drives to and from the hospital I talked to Sam about how I felt about using every possible means, not just the conventional routes, to bring about his good health. I explained that perhaps we needed to think about taking Essiac. The formula for making up the Essiac solution had arrived some time before and I had tried to persuade Sam then that it would be a good idea to take it. He was adamant that he would not swallow the stuff and I let the idea drop for the moment and hid the herbs away.

I didn't say it to Sam, but I was beginning to wonder what *was* going to achieve remission. We had almost exhausted what conventional medicine could offer us and I worried about the future constantly. Sam looked amazingly well but the leukaemia was still there. I felt we needed to look for other ways that maybe, just maybe, would give us what we wanted. Eventually Sam agreed to take the Essiac and from that point onwards he took the herbs three times a day. I must admit I wondered what on earth I was doing, as it came with very complicated instructions to follow and I would have to make vast brews at home and then bring it into the hospital for Sam. I was beginning to feel like a witch – albeit a well-meaning one!

It was always a battle as he didn't like the taste, but three times a day I brewed the solution up and he swallowed it after plenty of fuss and lots of bribery. I warmed the Essiac up in the parents' kitchen and the herb essence swept down the ward causing a few raised eyebrows. I had told the doctors that I was giving Sam Essiac because, despite my desire to do everything in my power to help Sam, I didn't want any of the more alternative avenues I was exploring to harm the treatment that Sam was receiving at the hospital. The doctors had no objections to the Essiac as the ingredients could not do him any harm.

This time the only problem Sam had as a side effect of the chemo were the high temperatures that had plagued him throughout his treatment. These, as usual, disappeared as soon as his marrow recovered. The doctors were all pleasantly surprised that the children seemed to tolerate FLAG so well, given that it was a relatively new course of medicine at the time. Now, it is good to see that FLAG is being used more routinely in the treatment of AML.

During this course we were still having regular healing from the Harry Edwards Healing Sanctuary (who specialised in absent healing), Betty Shine also sent absent healing, and of course, I carried on with the once a day treatment. Absent healing can be very beneficial and is a simple process whereby the healer will sit quietly and bring to mind the face (if a photo is available) or if not, the name of the patient, and then simply send love and light to the situation. Some healers who do this work ask for weekly reports so they can send the healing to the current problem if there is one. Though absent healing may sound strange and is definitely harder for anyone who is a sceptic about healing to believe, we found it very helpful and if no healer is available to come to the hospital it is certainly better than nothing. I thought to myself how wonderful it would have been if there had been healing available *in situ* on Robin Ward; it would have helped the children and parents so much. I considered myself very fortunate to know about this help when Sam became ill and to be able to use it to help him through his treatment.

The radionics was also an ongoing thing and so I felt quite satisfied that Sam was being helped as much as possible. Certainly for a boy who was on his fourth course of chemo he was in amazingly good health, and just seeing him so full of life was a bonus to us all. In comparison to other children he had more energy, fewer side effects from the treatment and a better appetite than most children being treated, all things that helped him and us as a family have a better quality of life.

It was during this fourth course of treatment that we met the consultant in charge of bone-marrow transplants, Paul Veys. If FLAG was successful and Sam was in remission we would be under his care for a transplant. Paul Veys was a breath of fresh air. His whole demeanour was one of hope and positive action and we left his office feeling completely uplifted. It reinforced my thoughts that doctors – while obviously having to tell you the truth however unpalatable that may be – should try never to rob a patient of hope, as hope is as essential to life as the breath that flows through us. It also showed me that for some doctors the combination of truth and hope was possible. Paul Veys never gave us false hope, but somehow made us feel that there were still options left for us, especially if Sam was in remission after this course of treatment.

We came out of hospital the following day to wait for an appointment in a week's time to have yet another aspirate test to see if Sam had achieved remission. I started to pray like I have never prayed before. I didn't know if there was a God out there listening or not, but I knew my mum was out there somewhere and I prayed to her to help Sam. I know that many people have found themselves in this position, but I think that my faith in healing and the other alternative therapies helped me to really believe that my prayers could help. After all, we needed Sam to be in remission and we needed it NOW!

CHAPTER 12

The days leading up to the testing of Sam's marrow were some of the longest of my life. So much depended on whether FLAG had been successful in putting Sam in remission; without the remission we could not go ahead with the transplant.

We were aware that we had the most enormous advantage in that Nick was a match for Sam. So many people wait in vain for a match to become available. The Anthony Nolan Trust was set up in 1974 by Shirley Nolan in memory of the life of her son Anthony who suffered with a rare bone-marrow disease. It was the first register of volunteers willing to donate bone marrow to those people who need a transplant but have no suitable donor within their family. Ashley Grice was one such boy. We met him in hospital on his third relapse. His mother Lyn was fighting like a tigress to get more donors to come forward. She had contacted the Duchess of York's charity Children in Crisis and the press were helping her with as much publicity as possible to encourage new donors to come on to the register with the hope that one of them would be a match for Ashley. She is an amazing woman and she has, through her efforts, brought thousands of new donors forward as a result of her fight for Ashley. Ashley did eventually receive an 'unrelated' transplant, which was a success; however, complications and infection tragically led to his death. We were in a privileged position compared to him and others like him.

We all drove up to Great Ormond Street for Sam to undergo his bone-marrow aspirate test. He seemed less terrified this time, perhaps sensing the importance of the day. We had decided not to wait around the hospital, but to hear the results over the phone. I wanted to be safe at home so that, whatever the result, we could come to terms with it in the privacy of our own home.

Sam recovered quickly from the procedure and we made our way home through the busy London traffic. The anxiety was apparent in every thing we did – David's driving was appalling and my face in the mirror of the passenger visor seemed to age in front of my eyes. The boys seemed to be the only ones who remained calm, bickering normally in the back of the car.

It was at these dreadful 'crunch' times that the knowledge that we were using so many other supportive treatments for Sam helped me to carry on.

The phone rang at about four that afternoon. My heart jumped into my mouth and David picked up the phone. I could hear him talking in a level voice, giving no clue to what was being said. When he hung up he looked at me and said, 'The leukaemia stands at 4 per cent.'

I don't think he realised what he had said, as there was no reaction on his part at all. The boys and I went potty, though, dancing around the room chanting, 'Remission, remission!'

I asked him what else the registrar had said and David replied that he couldn't remember, he had gone into a complete daze with the excitement of the news. When I rang back and spoke to the registrar we discussed what to do next, which was to have another dose of FLAG to consolidate the remission and then plan for a transplant as soon as possible.

We had the most wonderful weekend, going out to our favourite restaurant with the boys to celebrate and ringing around the family giving them the good news. Hope had been handed to us at last and it felt absolutely wonderful.

The following week we returned to the hospital to have a further dose of FLAG. Again the reaction from the nursing staff was heart-warming; people seemed delighted for us. Our consultant smiled and seemed pleased, but left us slightly deflated with the remark that we would have to see how Sam was after the next course of chemo before going ahead with the transplant.

To be fair to him and others like him, I realise that many years of dealing with seriously sick children must make you a little pessimistic, but I still totally believe that without hope you leave parents and patients with nothing to cling to, which in the end makes the doctors' job that much harder. We all have the same goal, after all, which is to get the children well again.

Most of our pals had left the ward by now, the only exception being a delightful little girl called Amy. Little Amy was also chasing a remission and her brother was a match for her. Amy's mum and I hoped to be on the transplant side of the ward together. It was a devastating blow to hear that she had not obtained remission and that there was nothing more the doctors could do for her. It was heartbreaking to say goodbye knowing that, but for a miracle, Amy would pass over in just a few weeks. To have our chance and for Amy to be robbed of hers was very hard to bear for all of us.

It was about this time that David was made redundant. Friends were horrified for us, but I thought it was perfect timing as now David would be able to be with us more. He had a very difficult role to fulfil, trying to work, keep Nick happy and still visit Sam whenever he could. David said that he felt relieved at the time – the redundancy gave us money to live on for the next year and gave him a breathing space. I knew that David found life very stressful both physically and mentally, and I hoped that some of his stress could be reduced by the unexpected changes in his working life.

We would certainly be finding it more difficult when Sam was in isolation having his transplant, and I reasoned that arrangements would be far easier now that David was to be unemployed!

We were allowed home for a week's break to enable Sam to get his strength back before the transplant. We decided to travel up to Blakeney in Norfolk for a long weekend; we had spent many summer holidays up in Norfolk and hoped to recapture some of those happy memories. We had a wonderful time, and the Norfolk winds certainly blew some cobwebs away. Sam and Nick fished for crabs and flew kites on the deserted beaches.

While we were there we visited Walsingham. Pilgrims come from all over the world to visit the Shrine of Our Lady of Walsingham, as it has a reputation that healing miracles have taken place there. We were lucky enough to visit while a healing service was in progress and Sam was sprinkled with the water from the well, said to have special healing properties. Sam didn't think much of the whole thing – being sprinkled with water from a well was a step too far for him! For me it was simply a question of 'It can't hurt and it may even help'.

We went into a local pub for a coffee afterwards and noticed hanging on the wall a picture of Gary Lineker's family. They had also visited Walsingham during their son George's treatment for leukaemia. It felt good to know we were following in their footsteps, as George is now fit and well. We left Norfolk refreshed and ready to go into hospital, eager to get on with the transplant. First, though, we needed to celebrate the boys' birthdays – Nick's was first, on 13 April, followed by Sam's the following day. We had been warned that Sam would most likely not be feeling well enough to celebrate in hospital, as he would have received his conditioning chemotherapy by the time of his birthday, so we brought their birthday celebrations forward by a week. No complaints from the boys of course – double the fun again!

We had a lovely couple of days pushing the boat out and treating the boys to a pair of remote-control cars that they had always wanted. A few days later we packed to go into hospital for the transplant. We were so very glad to have the opportunity to hopefully cure Sam's illness, yet felt huge fear and trepidation at all that lay in front of us.

We were admitted to the bone-marrow transplant side of Robin Ward on Easter Monday 1996. It seemed a very appropriate date to me, as I felt a little as if we were having a rebirth of sorts, with the transplant. For the first five days we would be free to move in and out of our room freely. Then, as Sam's marrow would be bombarded by the conditioning treatment to prepare for Nick's marrow, we would have to move to another (isolation) room that had been especially prepared for the remainder of our treatment.

At that point, as Sam would be in isolation, we would only be able to have either David or myself in the room with him. The exception to this was one other named person – we had chosen one of the healers, Kim, to be that named person. He had agreed to come up to the hospital to give Sam healing (and me as well if I needed it). Kim came once or twice a week during that period and I continued to give healing once a day. I felt I could do no more – we were all doing everything that we could.

Nick could not be allowed into the room until Sam's counts had recovered, as he would be a possible source of infection to Sam. This was the only thing that Sam was really upset about and it was very hard for him to accept the separation.

Our first day back in hospital was taken up with finding out the transplant ward's routine and learning the hygiene and feeding procedures necessary to protect Sam once he was in isolation.

The conditioning chemotherapy started that night and I slept badly (this was unknown territory to me); however, Sam slept peacefully and apart from some nausea felt fine. The chemo obviously had a cumulative effect, however, and by the fifth day Sam was feeling very sick with a lot of stomach cramps and sickness. I alerted the radionics practitioner and hoped that the therapy would be as effective as it had been in the past. The stomach cramps eased off a few hours after I had alerted the practitioner, another indicator to me of how effective the treatment was.

The first day Sam was to be in isolation was Nick's birthday. Sam's room had been prepared in advance for him with a special cleaning regime, and the play specialist had kindly left lots of new toys to welcome Sam into the room. Sam was allowed a few of his special toys from home and a few special teddy bears – they had to be washed and sealed in plastic bags for the journey to the hospital to ensure we carried no germs or bacteria into the room. This was all done to hopefully make the isolation easier, and it was an adventure for the first five minutes, but then the reality of Nick sitting outside the cubicle and Sam being inside in isolation hit home and Sam cried bitterly.

We soon realised that it only made matters worse for Sam to see Nick and not to be able to touch him and play with him. We had a family conference and decided it would be better for both the boys to have Nick visit less often during this stage of isolation. We were lucky enough to have a phone in the room that linked to the corridor outside and so they made do with phoning each other whenever they liked.

Now that Sam was in isolation whoever entered the room had to change footwear and wash their hands on entering and leaving; we also had to wear a plastic apron to protect Sam from germs. He had his own cook who prepared meals for him under strictly controlled conditions. David and I had to eat our meals in the corridor as an extra safeguard.

The day following our move into isolation was Sam's birthday. As anticipated, he didn't feel well enough to celebrate, but the staff did their best to cheer him up by gathering around the window outside his room singing 'Happy Birthday' – we all promised ourselves that next year would be better.

The transplant day was booked for 19 April. Nick appeared very calm about the whole procedure, but as the transplant day approached he said he would feel happier to be with us all at the hospital, so we arranged for him to have time off school.

The evening before transplant Nick was admitted onto the same ward as Sam. It was very emotional to have both my children in hospital. Seeing Nick looking so vulnerable and very much a young boy – although he had just had his thirteenth birthday – I was struck by the awesome task he was undergoing to help his brother. David and I spent the night in hospital, one in each room. I don't think either of us had much sleep that night, although the boys both slept soundly.

The following morning Nick did feel quite nervous and so the doctors gave him a temazepam to help calm his nerves. After the drug had taken effect Nick was nicer to me than he had been for many a year! David took Nick down to the theatre while I sat with Sam. I knew that the procedure would take about an hour and a half and the time passed slowly. By the end of the ninety minutes I was pacing up and down the ward. After what seemed like an age we were called to say that Nick was ready to be collected. It was my turn to go to theatre and I was very relieved to see Nick all in one piece – just a bit sleepy.

As we came back onto the ward Sam's nose was pressed against his cubicle window to catch a glimpse of Nick as he was taken back to his room. Only a few hours later Sam was receiving Nick's marrow via his Hickman line. It was wonderful seeing the marrow from Nick dripping slowly into Sam. Hope in a bag!

CHAPTER 13

Nick felt a little sick from the anaesthetic but was otherwise fine; he recovered quickly and was able to play computer games from his bed. The beds are child-sized and Nick had the body of a large teenager, which meant his feet hung out of the end of the bed! Nick went home the next day; I think people generally have the feeling that giving marrow is an unpleasant and debilitating thing to do, but nothing could have been further from the truth for Nick. Others may have a less easy time giving their marrow but for Nick it was not a problem – in fact, he was fit enough to run for his school team a few days later, and we all cheered delightedly when he won!

The transplant had been completed, Nick's marrow was now in Sam and all we could do was wait and hope that Sam would not develop any life-threatening infections during the time that he had no functioning marrow of his own to protect him. The purpose of the transplant was to knock Sam's marrow for six with the conditioning treatment, then introduce Nick's marrow via the transplant. The idea was for Nick's marrow to take over and re-educate Sam's marrow to work normally. It was one of those things that if you said it quickly seemed no problem at all!

We now had the long wait for Sam's counts to recover and the anxiety of seeing which marrow would recover first. Sam was beginning to suffer from the effects of the chemo and felt uncomfortable enough to have some Oramorph (liquid morphine) to help with the pain. It is common for the intensive treatment to destroy the lining of your mouth and gut, and it was for this problem that the liquid morphine was given.

We had one dreadful day when the staff insisted on Sam being fitted with a morphine pump that he could, in theory, operate himself to control any pain he was having. I was persuaded against my better judgment to let Sam have the pump fitted, which meant Sam having to be held down while we inserted the needle into his arm. Sam had his own way of dealing with the pump. His arm swelled alarmingly and the needle had to be taken out later that day. The next day he was much better, as if to prove to us that he had not needed the pump at all.

Our healer, Kim, was making regular visits to us during our time in isolation. It was a great comfort to me to know that Sam had so much support coming from so many different sources. I developed a heavy cold, possibly as a reaction to the stress of the situation. I managed to hide the fact that I had a cold from the staff, as I would not have been allowed in the room if they had known. I believed that for Sam to be without me at that point would have been far more harmful than the risk of his catching a cold. Not everyone reacts in the same way in each situation and to some people this course of action might seem irresponsible. However, as a parent it felt right to me at the time. Sam and I hid behind the curtains until the cold had passed and luckily he had no adverse effects from my cold.

The following week Sam felt very tearful and ill and the isolation also began to have an effect on me. Sam put the situation beautifully by pointing out that I could leave the cubicle at any time while he could not. I could only help him by trying to focus on the future and encourage him to look forward to the day when he would be able to get the long-awaited puppy. I asked those healers who were sending absent healing to Sam to include me in their thoughts too.

The days passed very slowly and we moved an exercise bike into our room to motivate Sam and indeed myself, and to increase his cell count. Paul Veys had told Sam that exercise was very good for him and so Sam peddled away morning and evening.

May arrived and I hoped that we would not have to wait too

much longer to see some movement in the blood counts. I was rewarded the very next day with our first healthy white cell!

Our pleasure was short-lived, however, as Sam started to show signs of Graph-versus-Host Disease (GVHD). The doctors actually wanted a degree of GVHD because it was assumed that this was a sign that Nick's healthy marrow was fighting Sam's. Too much, though, could be potentially life threatening as the disease could affect the major organs. Sam's GVHD seemed to affect his stomach and gave him a rash. This was uncomfortable for him but not a major problem. We spent a miserable few days with Sam having to rush to the loo every few hours and he became quite despondent.

I approached our consultant to see if we could allow Nick into the room to cheer Sam up and he agreed that it would be beneficial. It was a wonderful moment to see Sam's face light up as Nick came through the door. They hugged for a few moments and then got stuck into the serious business of playing the new computer game that Sam had in the room. Sam had written to Virgin Megastores asking for a Play Station to be donated to the ward so that people like him would find it easier to be in hospital. They were very generous and sent the ward one almost immediately.

Now that Nick was allowed into the room the time seemed to go much more quickly and Sam seemed to improve daily. The drugs that Sam had been having through his Hickman line to prevent infection and rejection of Nick's marrow were now being changed to an oral regime, which was the first step towards being discharged. The next morning Paul Veys, after checking Sam over, uttered those magic words: 'Sam, how would you like to go home next week?'

At last!

The following days were hectic. Now that Sam was coming home the house had to be cleaned as it had never been cleaned before. As far as possible it had to be a dust-free area for Sam; every teddy bear had to be washed and all bed linen and all soft furnishings around the house had to be washed and tumble-dried. Nothing could be put out in the garden to dry in case of any bugs attaching themselves to the washing, so our house hummed with activity and the sounds of the washing machine and the drier!

Back on the ward it was no less busy. The dietician came to give me advice on what to give Sam to eat, and how to prepare foods to avoid the risk of infection. He would no longer have his own cook and would have to make do with family cooking once again; we would have to make the adjustment carefully.

Sam was now allowed out of his room at night to play pool but his contact with people had still to be kept to a minimum for his own safety. I thought Sam would not want to return to his room after being allowed out but, to my surprise, he was more than happy to return. He felt very strange being outside the four walls that had been his world for the past six weeks. He soon acclimatised though and became more confident each day.

Eventually, in late May 1996, the day came to leave. We had made a cake for the staff and we packed our room up in a daze, hardly daring to believe we were about to leave the hospital for the last time after eight months. Sam would be back the following week, but only as an out-patient, which was a wonderful feeling. Sam had a large number of tablets to take every day but he would be weaned off them slowly and eventually he would not need any drugs at all. There were a few damp eyes around that day from some of the staff who had become firm friends, also from myself at the huge sense of relief that after all the traumas of the past months we were about to walk out of the hospital. So many of our friends, including Harry, had not been so lucky.

We were waved off in fine style and drove home, our hearts happy for the first time in ages. There were no cast-iron guarantees for the future, but we were bringing home a healthy boy thanks to the skill of the staff at Great Ormond Street Hospital and, without any doubt at all, the love and help from the many healers and therapists who had given so generously of their time and energies.

I believe *all* the therapies we used had been of benefit, but over the months some stood out as having had a profoundly positive effect when Sam's journey had become difficult. For me it seemed that healing, both absent and hands-on, along with the radionics, were invaluable tools for us to use alongside the conventional medicine that was on offer. I had seen Sam respond dramatically to both of those therapies when he was very ill with stomach problems, and was convinced that they had made a vital difference to his wellbeing, both physically and emotionally. The nursing staff also made the most enormous difference to our quality of life; their cheerful, caring approach to our family was a healing gift in itself. Despite all the terrible odds with Sam's disease and complications of his subtype, we had survived the experience and I was sure that if healing was available on units such as this other patients might find their quality of life could be improved too.

That idea would have to wait for the future, though, as all I wanted to do at that time was go home and be a family again.

CHAPTER 14

Sam was no longer an in-patient but the reality was that he would be back the following week for his regular clinic appointments at the hospital. This would be a blood test to check for any sign of the leukaemia returning and to monitor the many pills and potions that still had to be taken to protect Sam from the outside world.

Some of the medication was to help the new bone marrow from Nick to engraft until eventually Sam would be free of all the medication. Sam was always very keen to tell people that he took a total of 77 pills each day! In reality the amount was less than that but, by the time we had broken the pills into a more convenient size for Sam to swallow, there were indeed 77 pieces.

To visit the hospital once a week was of course a major milestone and we had dreamed of reaching this point. There was a vague sense of disbelief that first day at being home as a family, and we had been warned by various people who had trod this road before us that things would be difficult for a while as we all adjusted to our new routine. In fact, we never looked back apart from that first day, and just loved the freedom that being at home gave us. We quickly adapted to our old lifestyle and fell back into the old family patterns. It was a novelty at first to be in charge of all the washing and ironing and all the other chores that go with being a normal mother and housewife, but I have to confess the novelty quickly wore off!

In our first week at home it was only too apparent that Sam was not well; he developed a fever that resulted in us rushing up to the hospital. It was a shock when Sam felt really ill as he had gone through very harsh treatments during his time in hospital without any real problems – to see him so obviously unwell was frightening.

It was with heavy hearts that we all waited anxiously while the doctors examined Sam. As suspected, the problem was an infection of the Hickman line. This was a fairly common occurrence for children with a Hickman line fitted, but Sam had never been troubled with one before. He was started on a course of several weeks of intravenous antibiotics immediately; he quickly stabilised and began to feel better within hours. The nurses taught me how to mix and administer the drugs he would need at home and we set off from the hospital as soon as possible, anxious to distance ourselves from the medical environment.

An appointment was made for the following week to take the Hickman line out so that for the first time in almost a year Sam would be free of a line hanging out of the middle of his chest. The most important result of this according to him was that he could now have a bath without me – he was very pleased!

The line infection had been a scare for us, and an unwelcome reminder that we were still far from the normal family we would have liked to be. However, in our attempt to return to a 'normal' life, David began to attend a series of interviews. It was to be more than a year before David was employed again but I know that he valued that time at home with Sam during that first year after the bone-marrow transplant. Sam's risk of infection with his lowered immune system was too great for him to begin school straightaway so he was still able to avoid it and he had a home tutor. Mr Sharpe was a gentle man with a great sense of humour and Sam enjoyed spending time with him. I don't think much school work was done but it was a gentle reminder of what normal life was like; it also meant that I could take one of my hats off (schoolteacher) and just be a mum again. However, I didn't take off my healer hat. Over a period of time we reduced all the other therapies such as the radionics and the Essiac (I would dearly have loved Sam to continue taking it but he really didn't want to, saying the taste was disgusting and he didn't need it any more because he was better), but the healing carried on, as I was sure that Sam would continue to benefit from the supportive care that I believed healing could give him.

There were some very happy times for Sam in that first year post-transplant. One of the happiest was the news that the Jack Russell puppy that was to be his had been born and could be collected from Wiltshire in a matter of weeks. We checked with the hospital that it was OK for Sam to have the puppy, which had by now been named Zack, and they gave their seal of approval. Without the Hickman line the risks of having a dog in the house were much the same as for any other child and they were happy for us to go ahead. Sam spent many hours poring over dog books, eager to ensure that his puppy had the best care possible. The day Zack the puppy arrived Sam became a devoted father and Zack and he became inseparable, spending many happy hours playing together.

Our appointments at the hospital had gradually been reduced from weekly, to fortnightly, and then monthly, which all helped to take the pressure off our nerves. Sam never talked to me about any anxiety he may have felt about the constant blood tests and I hope that for the most part I did the worrying for him. We would arrive at the day clinic for the blood test to be done, and then have to wait for several hours for the doctor's appointment and the results. We would chat away to nurses and fellow patients, outwardly looking calm, but inside I would be praying that everything was all right, and that we would be able to walk away from there in a few hours' time. I only ever felt like that at the hospital – when I was at home it was easier not to think about anything other than enjoying every day as it came. At the hospital, however, it was a different matter and my body would break into a sweat with the fear of what the results might bring.

I was still receiving healing myself, as I knew that the more I healed myself the more potent a healer I could become for Sam. I continued to read and research healers and healing. It is apparently a trap that most new healers fall into, that instead of channelling energy from outside themselves they are giving energy from their own energy supplies. If a healer continues to work in this way they will become exhausted and drained. Unless you are very disciplined, as a mother you are bound to fall into this trap. While I was receiving healing from other healers it was not a problem, as I would have my energy levels topped up. Now, though, I wanted to be as potent a healer as I could be and that meant getting more knowledge – a permanent solution rather than a temporary one.

I continued to see Kim as he lived in the same town as us, but Sam no longer wanted to be bothered to sit still for healing. He would tolerate it from me but only after a lot of bribery, and Essiac was a thing of the past as far as he was concerned. Despite my misgivings about stopping some of the alternative therapies we had been so reliant on, I had to accept that he must be able to choose for himself now that he was well again.

CHAPTER 15

Over the next few months, as life settled down, we decided to move house in an attempt to leave the unhappiness behind, and began to view different properties. The boys found all this very exciting; bigger rooms for them and a larger garden for the puppy to play in. Life seemed to be picking up and Sam began to go out to his best friend Tom's house for tea again. Tom had always been a great support to Sam, visiting the hospital regularly, and it was wonderful to see them running around together again, eating their favourite meal of pizza and chips with plenty of vinegar!

Nick and Sam had reverted to their usual brother-type relationship, quite competitive but very loving. Nick was now thirteen and a half and was growing up fast; he was very like David in that he did not want to talk about his feelings. Sam and I continued to have occasional Alex-times. We both enjoyed these sessions and they gave me a chance to see how Sam was in a rather more emotional way. Sam would often bring up his dislike of school and we made no move to persuade him to return. I wanted Sam to make the decision about that himself and if he never wanted to go back into mainstream education, I felt sure we could find an alternative.

I was surprised, therefore, at the end of the summer holidays in 1996 when Sam suddenly decided that he would like to attempt returning to school. He said he was not looking forward to it but in his own mind he felt that going back to school meant he was like other children again, and he forced himself to go. It was hard for

Sam and it was very hard for me. I had spent the last year hardly leaving his side and now I had to let him walk away from me into school – I shed many tears when I got home that first day.

Sam settled into his new routine, firstly going for half a day and then a full day. The school had been warned that the chickenpox virus was a major danger to Sam; if he came into contact with the virus he would be at risk of developing shingles which was potentially life threatening to him with his lowered immune system. All the parents at the school had been sent a memo to that effect but unfortunately within a few weeks there was a case of chickenpox at the school and Sam developed shingles.

The treatment for shingles when you are immune-suppressed is intravenous antibiotics. It was a nightmare; at the local hospital Sam had to have a cannula fitted into his small veins several times a day as the lines kept failing. It was actually worse than the chemotherapy had been. Sam was extremely upset and after all that we had been through it felt like the last straw. I think the only thing that kept Sam motivated was his puppy Zack waiting at home for him and the fact that we had a holiday booked to go to Cyprus in a few weeks' time.

Sam managed to recover from his shingles and we flew out to Cyprus in October – the sun and the sea helped Sam's spirits to recover. This was good news, but it was in Cyprus that I first began to realise that there were now some very large cracks appearing in our marriage. David and I were both aware of the changes but David was uncomfortable talking about issues that might threaten the status quo in our marriage. In reality we were both so relieved to have Sam well and for all of us to be on holiday together that we just buried the unrest and tried to carry on as normal. On the surface everything was the same, but I was now a very different person to the one I had been before Sam's diagnosis, and it showed in the relationship between David and myself. We had encountered our differences in earlier years, which had been papered over as all couples do, but now it seemed that we were in real trouble.

When Mum was diagnosed with cancer in 1987 I had read a lot of self-help manuals and spiritual books which had begun to show me a very different way of living and which had also opened my eyes to all the different alternative therapies that were available. The more I grew spiritually the more it became obvious that David and I were no longer on the same wavelength. However, I believed that children deserve both parents to be around for them as they grow and develop, and continued to believe that any difficulties would sort themselves out. I often thought to myself that when the children were older we would be in trouble but I pushed the thoughts away to be dealt with in the future.

We arrived back from Cyprus and the boys returned to school. Sam was not happy to be there but would always decline if I asked him if he would prefer a home tutor, as he wanted to try and be like the other boys. Hindsight is the clearest of vision and, had I known then what I know now about the mind–body link regarding stress, I would not have let him continue at school. I would also have been more forceful and insisted he took Essiac and continued with the healing. Though I had continued to give Sam the odd healing session when he came home from hospital, we had gradually stopped over the summer holidays. I have no way of knowing if doing those things would have made the vital difference but, looking back, I would have felt more confident if we had done. Still, Christmas was coming and that meant good times, very different to this time last year.

We had an important doctor's appointment at Great Ormond Street just before Christmas – a kind of MOT test after Sam's transplant. Sam passed all the tests with flying colours and we travelled home in great spirits, looking forward to the Christmas festivities. We had the most wonderful Christmas; everything seemed to be going our way again and we were all so happy to be well and home together again.

It was a particularly busy day at the clinic when we arrived for our checkup in February 1997 (Sam had been doing so well that we had been allowed to skip a month and go onto bi-monthly checks). David was back at work and Nick was in school, so these appointments were an opportunity for the two of us to have a treat in London together. We had arrived at the clinic at 10.00 a.m. and as the hours passed I became more and more uneasy, as it was unusual to have to wait a long time. By half past four in the afternoon Sam was understandably fed up with waiting and I felt an overwhelming desire to pick him up and rush out of the hospital. I think I must have known that something was not right, as my sense of panic grew and I fought to keep calm for Sam's sake. Eventually I was led into the doctor's room, leaving Sam playing on the computer.

I noticed straight away that there was a nurse in attendance. I knew this was a bad sign as I had learned over the past year that whenever there was bad news, a nurse would be present – my heart began to pound in my chest. The doctor came straight to the point and said Sam had some suspect cells in his blood. Pushing my mounting panic to one side I took a deep breath and said, 'What can we do about it?' She replied that there really was nothing much they could offer, as Sam's disease was so difficult to treat.

I recalled that when Sam was first diagnosed I had read about a procedure called donor lymphocyte infusions and had read that they may be of benefit if a relapse occurred. The treatment meant taking more cells from Nick and infusing them into Sam – this would essentially top up the original transplant and encourage Nick's marrow to work within Sam. The doctor said that she would confer with her colleagues and get back to us but, in principle, Sam could attempt the treatment. I left the room and fixed a reassuring smile on my face as I went out to collect Sam. He knew straight away that something was wrong, being no longer an innocent seven year old; he had been through a lot and had the wisdom of a much older person. I told him that a few nasty cells had returned and we would need an extra bit of treatment to get rid of them. He didn't seem too bothered. I found that if I presented information to him in a pragmatic way he usually accepted that everything was under control and there was nothing much for him to worry about.

We went home to tell Nick that his brother was still ill and that we had to come back into hospital and have more treatment. I was worried how Nick would take the news, as he had played such an important part in Sam's treatment by donating his marrow. I did not want him to think that what he had done was to no avail. Nick's response was as pragmatic as Sam's; he had seen many children on the ward relapse and he knew that some of them still recovered very well.

Nick asked me what he could do to help and I explained that we were looking into a procedure that may mean taking a bit more blood from him. Despite his fear of needles and me saying that he didn't have to do it, he wanted to do whatever he could to help Sam. David and I both wished that Nick did not have to make this decision and that one or the other of us could have donated the cells that Sam needed, but Nick was the only potential match. We had to come to terms with the fact that our boys had yet more trouble in store for them.

It was a shock to be right back at square one, but I consoled myself with the knowledge that we now had so many tried and tested tools at our disposal. Healing, radionics and Essiac could all be used again to help Sam get well from this relapse. I only wish we had never stopped using them in the first place. I didn't say so to my family, but I wondered if things might have been different if we had kept up with all the things that helped contribute to Sam getting well.

Doris, who had supplied me with the Essiac, had suggested it might be better to make Sam continue to take it. I will never know whether it would have helped or not, but I know if I had the same choice again I would insist that Sam continue with Essiac and healing. Some years later I read a book on healing that advised, 'when treating patients with leukaemia, you should advise your patients to have healing as a prophylactic measure'. It was felt to be important to remain vigilant with a damaged immune system. I certainly advise all my patients now to continue seeing a healer when they are well, even if it is only once a month; it may be one of the vital ingredients that keeps you well. I have no scientific proof that this is true, but it is what I intuitively feel and, given my experiences, these days I very much listen to my intuition.

CHAPTER 16

How did it feel to have the news of Sam's relapse? It felt like my heart and stomach had been ripped out. I'm sure it was equally painful for David but, once again, we didn't have the time or the desire to talk about it. Neither of us knew what to say to the other. David knew there was nothing he could say or do to make 'everything all right again', and in the way that men do he would have liked to 'fix' things. This must have made him feel very impotent. He had always found it difficult to talk about his feelings and this latest development was no exception. It would have been nice for me to have been able to support him but I had nothing left in my reserves to offer him. My mind was racing and my body hurt physically with the mental and emotional shock. Nick and Sam seemed to accept the news far better than the two of us.

We both turned inward with our terror and hurt. We knew that, on paper, now that Sam had relapsed he could potentially only have weeks to live. Very often the patient does not respond to treatment a second time, as the body has become used to the drugs and less sensitive to the treatment. Knowing this was one thing, but accepting it was a very different thing and I immediately set about contacting all the people that had been helpful to us before. I alerted all the healers who could send absent healing and spoke to the radionics practitioner, who asked for a new sample of Sam's hair to begin her work again.

One of the people that I rang was Lyn Grice, whom I had met at Great Ormond Street. Her son Ashley was also once again in a relapse situation and I contacted her to see how he was getting on. She told me that the Duchess of York (who had been helping Ashley find a donor via Children in Crisis) had introduced her to a holistic healer who had treated Ashley. Lyn recommended that I take Sam to see him as Ashley had enjoyed the treatment. My attitude to good health has always been that modern medicine can achieve a lot but it cannot do everything; therefore there are other ways to be explored that may help. I feel good health can be viewed as a jigsaw, and if you are ill some of the pieces are missing. To be well you need to keep searching until you have all the pieces in place, and it was for that reason that Sam was having a lot of complementary medicine alongside his conventional treatment.

Before we could seek out this new healer, however, Sam had an appointment booked for the following week to have a new Hickman line fitted before he could start his new treatment. The new donor lymphocyte procedure could only take place after Sam had received more chemotherapy to try and put him back into remission. Sam was initially reluctant to have a line fitted again, but eventually was persuaded that a line would be better for him than endless needles in his arm. Nick had been told this time the cells would be collected via his blood, rather than by taking more marrow. This would mean that he would be attached to a machine for several hours, while the relevant cells were separated off from Nick's blood for Sam. I know that some nurses feel that family members do these things against their will, and that families put donors under emotional pressure to donate cells. Nick was surprisingly eloquent and said that he would have found it impossible to do anything other than offer his blood. I believe, as with so many other issues of this nature, that the people within the family should be left to make their own decisions. No one but those inside the situation knows exactly what it feels like. It is easy to judge from the outside but the family usually know what's best for their own circumstances.

The course of chemotherapy planned for Sam was once again FLAG, the regime that had achieved a remission for him before his transplant. Sam had tolerated it very well before and we were hopeful that we would get a good result once again.

As the regime was so well tolerated we would be able to stay overnight and then go home for most of the day. This was good for Sam's morale as he could see Zack, and I could make sure he ate well at home. The course of treatment passed with no problems and once again the doctors were surprised by how well Sam was, despite his relapse.

Paul Veys had got used to 'the Buxtons' by now and could see that we were very capable as a family of taking care of Sam for the most part at home. I had been taught how to access his line to take blood for routine blood results. I then took the blood sample into our local hospital and rang for the results later that day, and any antibiotics Sam needed I was able to administer myself. All of this meant that Sam was able to be an out-patient for most of the time, which improved our quality of life enormously.

We made an appointment to see the healer that Ashley had seen, and drove down to his clinic in the leafy countryside of Surrey. Gareth was a very good advert for his holistic way of life; he was in his eighties but looked very much younger and was obviously very fit. He told us that he was up every morning at 5 a.m. in order to take cold baths and long jogs before starting his working day. Harry tested Sam's body and energy levels with a dowsing technique – we were all very intrigued by the pendulum he used to dowse with which used to swing madly in his capable hands – and he also took nail and hair samples to be sent away for analysis.

Some of the information Harry uncovered was quite extraordinary; for example, he said that amongst other things Sam had chemotherapy on his lungs, peroxide toxins, aluminium poisoning from cans, rubber and lead deposits, and told me that the measles jab that Sam had received as a young child had caused some problems with his bowels, which of course would not assist him to eliminate these things.

One of the fascinating things that Harry was able to uncover was that he could tell that Sam had received a knock to his head some years ago. I was able to check back over my diaries and what Harry said was true, right down to the month that he said it happened in.

Harry's method is that when he has the information he needs he places small tablets on the body and leaves them in place for some time to remove toxins that may be affecting the patient's ability to be well. We went to Harry for about six months, fitting in our appointments between conventional medicine. It is hard to say what concrete benefit there was for Sam, as Harry's methods were difficult for me to follow, but if nothing else we felt better by actively doing something to help ourselves. It was expensive seeing Harry, but at this point but we were fortunate to have money available to us that enabled us to follow this treatment.

When evaluating these things, I think it is important to remember that Sam was enjoying a good quality of life; in other similar children's cases, children were either in hospital, getting various infections or had even passed away into spirit. Sometimes complementary treatments are not so much about a cure but about quality of life and are well worth using for the precious extra time you have with your loved ones. As parents it was important to us that we tried all avenues that felt appropriate to us. However, I do think it is important to be cautious when going to therapists who charge huge amounts of money for their therapies. The Royal College of Nursing offers useful guidelines for patients who are interested in accessing complementary therapies. Once again, I thought how wonderful it would be if therapies were available on the NHS – it would save so much effort on behalf of the patient who may not have the energy to search for this complementary help as we were doing.

We always made these trips to the various therapists fun, taking sweets and drinks in the car and often stopping at Heathrow airport to watch the planes on the way home. When it was school holidays Nick would come too and we had a good time despite our situation; we travelled many miles to various therapists over the following year and it was always quality time where we enjoyed each other's company.

CHAPTER 17

We took the boys along to University College Hospital in London (UCLH had the latest equipment available for the procedure) for our appointment to harvest the cells that Nick was donating to Sam. By coincidence Stephen Rowley, who had nursed Sam at Great Ormond Street Hospital, now worked there and he came down to the unit to visit us all. Stephen took Sam away to look at computers and to introduce him to some pretty nurses (both hobbies they had in common!). David, Nick and I waited for the doctors to come along and the procedure to begin. It should have been a straightforward thing to achieve; Nick would have a needle inserted into his arm and the special machine would do the rest. Unfortunately Nick's veins completely disappeared when the doctors arrived, probably due to his needle phobia, making it impossible to achieve the harvest we needed. Nick became very pale and distressed and after several attempts we decided to call a halt and try again another day.

The following week the doctors tried again in the more familiar surroundings of Great Ormond Street and this time I sat with Nick giving him healing throughout the three hours he was on the machine. The cells were harvested without any trouble and were then infused into Sam via the Hickman line. I now know that the healing helped because the body relaxes during a healing session and the veins come to the surface of the skin. When you are frightened the opposite effect occurs. I have seen this happen many times since working on the unit at UCLH. This is one of the many situations where healing can be of use on an acute-care ward.

Nick seemed really pleased to have helped once again and Sam was always delighted to have in his words, 'a bit of his brother in him'. He used to joke that Nick's cells made him grumpy if he ever had a bad day, but I noticed a real closeness developing between them as Nick did more and more to help Sam. I did try, though, to make it very clear to Nick that this was just another way of helping Sam and there was no guarantee of success.

During this time we had moved into our new house, a lovely family home with a beautiful garden. David loved it; for him it was everything he had ever wanted in a house and he said to me while looking around the garden, 'Are you happy here?' I looked at him in disbelief as I was still feeling that I didn't think I would ever be happy again. It was nobody's fault, but another sign of how far apart we had grown. My weeks were filled with taking Sam's blood to check if his marrow was responding to the new treatment. I don't think you realise how far you are growing away from each other under these circumstances; bills need to be paid and David had to go to work, but he inhabited a very different world to mine.

Throughout the summer of 1997 Sam had regular infusions of Nick's cells. Many patients undergo this form of treatment and it is not always successful. However, we also had another weapon or two in our armoury and I continued to heal Sam and he continued to take Essiac – for us, thankfully, it was successful at keeping the disease stable. This is not a common state of affairs.

We spent a lot of time going for long walks with Zack, taking trips to the seaside, and lots of family outings during Nick's school holidays. The most wonderful thing we noticed was that Sam had more energy than all of us put together, he would often run up hills while the rest of us puffed up behind him. I believe that the therapies he was having helped him to tolerate the treatments; hand in hand, conventional and complementary treatments were achieving the good health he was enjoying.

During this time I attended my first official healing course. At the beginning I had been quite happy to give healing to family and friends and practise on people within my development group, but as before I wanted to make sure I was giving Sam the best healing that I could. I had been using other healers as well as myself in case I was missing something, but now I felt the time was right to attend a formal course. Up until now I had simply been visualising light entering my head and then travelling down my arms and into Sam. I wanted to know if there was anything I could improve upon.

The National Federation of Spiritual Healers is a nondenominational healing organisation for spiritual healers in Great Britain with a membership of about 6,000. It was founded in 1954 and is a registered charity, running regular healing courses for anyone interested in healing. (I have included their address at the back of the book for reference.)

I believe that when you are sad or ill one of the basic human needs is to feel the touch of a hand, but the federation teaches you to heal off the body and hardly touch at all. (When I am healing I work on and off the body as I believe both are important.) I came away with more questions than answers (questions such as: Is it really OK not to touch the body when healing? Am I the best person to give Sam healing or should I be looking for other healers for him? Does it have to be this complicated or is it a simple process as I believe it to be?) but the course filled in some gaps in my knowledge and taught me to heal without attachment. This means that you must try not to 'will' the patient better; you give healing in the knowledge that whatever happens is in the best interests of the patient, and you must trust in the process without trying to control it. Quite a tough one when it is your own child that you are trying to give healing to, but one I definitely needed to be aware of. Having taken Sam to several other healers it was interesting to see the different ways of laying on of hands. Some healers worked as the NFSH recommend, completely off the body, only touching the body if there is a physical pain to be healed. Others I had seen work completely on the body, moving their hand to specific positions. Still others lay hands on the patient's head or in one specific place and don't move for the whole length of treatment. I decided there was really no right or wrong way, only what was comfortable for your patient and yourself and, more importantly, what seemed to give the best results for my patients. Sometimes when I am working on the ward I am not able to touch the physical body at all because of an infection, so I do the whole session in the way that NFSH were teaching, but the patient will still feel the warmth from my hands and the positive effects of relaxation. At other times the patient will be able to be touched and will comment that there is nothing nicer than being touched by someone who doesn't have a needle in their hands. Occasionally I attend 'Mind, Body, Spirit' shows and see healers working while they make extraordinary noises with their breath! I don't think the NHS would go for that one yet! However, I still believe that whatever the technique healers are using we all have one thing in common, and that is we are all working with energy. However, there are many ways that a healer can become more effective, such as the ability to work intuitively and to add self-help techniques that can really help change a patient's negative patterns that may be contributing to their problems. My healing at home is certainly more comprehensive than the simple channelling of energy.

CHAPTER 18

In September 1997, both Sam and Nick had started the new term at school when once again, without any warning, the leukaemia escalated with a vengeance.

We were devastated; despite all our efforts the disease had taken hold again. For a day I wept, completely inconsolable. I found it impossible to keep up the mask that I usually had in place for the boys. Sam and Nick just put it down to Mum having a bad day and by the following morning I had recovered sufficiently to think more positively about what to do next. Sam had not been in remission this past year but the disease had been static, and I was sure the healing and other therapies had been responsible for keeping it like that. But now the leukaemia had become active again – why?

My faith in healing hadn't been shaken, as healing up to this point had been wonderful and had undoubtedly helped keep Sam's disease stable. He wasn't stable now, however, and we would probably be undergoing new untried conventional medicine – so to me it made sense to try different healers. The doctors used to view the different chemotherapy treatments as tools; if one combination had no effect they would try another. I viewed the different healers in the same way.

Once again we had to face the terror of the illness escalating. The fear was worst in the middle of the night, when terrifying dreams of me running up a mountain with Sam in my arms screaming for someone to help me would come repeatedly. I began to sleep lightly, as you do with a small baby, awaking at the slightest murmur from

Sam's bedroom. I felt that if I cracked, the whole family would fall apart. This was probably true in part – the Jewish faith has a saying that if the woman is strong the whole family will be well, and rightly or wrongly I felt it was up to me to be strong for everyone.

Despite the blood tests showing that Sam was once again dangerously ill he remained, in himself, very well. Once again I approached consultant Paul Veys for advice. We discussed giving Sam interferon, which I had read could be helpful, and Paul agreed that we could try it, warning me that Sam might feel quite unwell as interferon can give flu-like symptoms. The drug had to be given via an injection and I learned how to do this myself at home. It was not easy injecting my own child, but it cut out the long hours waiting at the hospital for a simple two-minute procedure and Sam was happy for me to do it. He tolerated the interferon very well and, thanks to the healing and radionics he was receiving, once again escaped most of the unpleasant side effects that could have impaired his quality of life.

Whenever I was desperate as I was again now, it seemed that out of nowhere a new source of healing became available to us; for whatever reason, three new healers came into our lives at this time. Sam was receiving healing several times a week from me but I felt healing from an outside source could still be helpful to us. A parent that we had met at the hospital heard that Sam was in trouble and rang to tell me that she was taking her son Jamie, who had a brain tumour, to a healer in Suffolk. I was aware of Matthew Manning's work as I had read some of his books, and when I rang for an appointment I was told his client list was full. We were put on a waiting list and his secretary told me that she would ring with the first available appointment. This was a bit of a blow, as I knew that time was of the essence for Sam, but we had no choice other than to wait.

The second healer who came to my attention I read about in a newspaper. Someone had apparently had a tumour that had been moved from an inoperable position into an operable position with the help of this man. I thought that if the healer could do that, he must be worth a try for Sam. You might think that Sam would be getting fed up with all these different people, but he was always happy to try something new, in his words 'to beat those white cells back' (leukaemia is a disease of the white cells and a vast amount of abnormal white blast cells was an indicator of the leukaemia being active again).

Sam was the most extraordinary boy, old beyond his years with a wisdom and happiness that touched everybody he met. He was certainly sometimes very naughty, telling inappropriate jokes to consultants and friends alike; adults would often say that talking to Sam was a revelation! I set about trying to track down this healer.

However, I had a third name that I could try – Charles Siddle, who had been recommended to us by a friend. Charles looked rather like a friendly grandfather, a small man with a shock of white hair and a white beard. Charles was not very good at communicating with his clients but, as he worked as an animal healer, this wasn't really a problem and to Sam it was a definite plus as he enjoyed taking his turn in the queue next to a cat, mouse or dog. Charles worked from a vet's surgery and his human clients had the luxury of sitting on a small stool within the surgery. On our first visit I wondered if I had gone too far this time. Sam sat there making funny faces at me while Charles laid his hands on him and did what seemed like a lot of huffing and puffing! Nevertheless, Sam felt very hot, which we took as a good sign.

After a lot of detective work I managed to trace the telephone number of the healer from the newspaper article, and we had booked an appointment to see him in a few weeks' time at a house in London. When we arrived for our first appointment, Sam was less than happy to find the sessions involved talking about emotions and feelings before the session of hands-on healing.

Sam wasn't impressed by all the talking, but during our appointment it occurred to me that I could benefit from this kind of healing. I was already aware of the mind–body link when it came to health. This link is the belief that whatever event affects us emotionally could eventually manifest in a physical problem at some point in the future; a lot of stress-related problems can be understood in this way. My mother had died of ovarian cancer and

I was already on the scanning programme at St George's Hospital in Tooting. This was as a precautionary measure, as my sister and I were considered high risk for the disease due to our family history. Hearing what this healer had to say made me think about my own health and I agreed to make an appointment for myself the following week.

My appointment lasted two hours and I wept for the whole of that time. I think I wept for everything that had happened over the past two years as well as before – going way back to my childhood. While you are releasing all of these emotions, you are very vulnerable and it is important to feel you are safe. I felt safe with this healer and as a consequence of the work we did, he knew more about me after those appointments than most other people ever had. I had never talked about those feelings to anyone. It was tough work uncovering all those issues about myself with everything else going on but the healer encouraged me to continue, saying that Sam would benefit from this 'new mum' that was being created. We would also often talk about my own healing abilities and how I could use them in the future.

After several months of treatment I decided that, for the moment, I would have to call a halt to my sessions – I could not afford any more and felt I had come to the end of what I could usefully do at that time. It was then that the healer said that I could continue my sessions without any further payment, saying that he enjoyed our appointments and the time we spent together. Given the strength I felt I was gaining from these sessions, though I was surprised at the offer, I agreed.

CHAPTER 19

In hindsight it seems so obvious what was happening, and I suppose I should have seen it coming, but over the preceding months I had willingly trusted the man I saw as my therapist. So when he told me that he knew of a way to increase the amount of energy I could channel into Sam, of course I asked him how. He said that by sleeping together it would open up my energy centres and make me a better channel for healing. My response was to laugh, and say that neither his wife nor my husband would think that was a good idea! He said that it was nothing to do with feelings, just energy, and I looked at him in astonishment – the healer that I trusted was suggesting a sexual act could help me to help my child. If I believed what he was saying and slept with him, I would have to live with the fact that I had done so while my son was sick and I was married, and if I did not, then I would always wonder if sleeping with him would have made a difference.

I left his house that day totally confused and shocked. A rational person who was not in my position would probably have reacted differently, but I felt trapped. Sam was still having sessions with this healer, so if I walked away and no longer took Sam to see him it may have been closing a door that was helping him. I didn't want to take that risk but neither did I want to continue seeing the healer. After much agonising, I decided to no longer see him and saw more of healer Matthew Manning instead. You can help protect yourself from this kind of person if you access healers from a recognised body (see the back of the book for details). I did write several letters to this healer's governing body to complain at his behaviour but incredibly I never received a proper reply – unsurprisingly the group that this healer was registered with is now defunct.

It was during dark moments such as this that I began to wonder if Sam really was going to pass away. Sam and I spent many hours travelling back and forth to out-patient appointments and healers. Often, during those bleak times of relapse, I would wonder whether it would be better just to drive off the road and end it all. I thought at least that way Sam and I would be together. There was only one problem with this idea, and that was Nick. How could I leave him? It must be bad enough having a sick brother without suddenly losing a brother and a mother. I never mentioned my idea to anyone, but I went over and over in my mind the ways that I could do the best for both of my children – in the end, of course, I did nothing. There was nothing to be done except to keep on keeping on. Sam would have been really angry if he had known what I was thinking; he never once felt like giving up and so it was my role to support him in whatever way I could and that is what kept me going.

The interferon injections kept the leukaemia stable for a few months but once again Sam's blood tests began to show an increase in leukaemia cells. We arranged another consultation with Paul Veys and decided to be admitted into hospital for a course of chemotherapy. The hoped-for result was that this would put Sam into remission and we would then be able to try a different type of transplant. These decisions were never just taken for Sam; he was always involved and very much made up his own mind about whether to have more treatment or not.

We went into hospital at the beginning of December and once again Sam remained well throughout the heavy chemotherapy. He even demonstrated press-ups to the doctors to persuade them that he was well enough to go home! On Christmas Eve Sam had another bone-marrow aspirate test to see if he was in remission or not. Waiting for results is one of the hardest things to deal with – your whole life hangs in the balance, the results will either give you hope or devastate you and your family. Here we were on Christmas

Eve, a special time, a time of hope and new beginnings and I was praying hard for a miracle, asking Mum once again to help.

The staff always took a great deal of care to make the ward look cheerful at Christmas and it really looked festive and bright that day. The children ran up and down the ward in high spirits despite their Hickman lines, medicine pumps and naked little heads; if you thought about them and all that they were going through, it became too much to bear, so we all pretended everything was fine and hid behind our masks.

The doctors arrived on the ward with Sam's results – he was not in remission. The leukaemia had not been affected at all by the treatment. It was terrible news, and there were several other patients on the ward who received bad news that day. It was a torturous time for all the parents. I have no doubt that it was also a bad day for the staff; some of them had become very fond of Sam and loved his amazing spirit and they were obviously very disappointed.

When the news was given to us, Sam looked at me without any outward signs of distress and said, 'We'd better go home for Christmas then, Mum.' That's exactly what we did and the next day we opened our presents and went off to my sister-in-law's for a big family celebration. Sam kept us all amused by his antics and his high energy. The expression 'There are many tears in the heart that never reach the eyes' was very appropriate for all of us that day. Nick was very quiet but did not want to talk about his feelings. I could see that he was angry inside but I felt powerless to help him with the anger. He did not want to receive healing at that time, only choosing to access help after Sam had passed away.

The New Year arrived and I wondered what 1998 would have in store for us. I never allowed myself to dwell on the possibility that Sam might not make it. We lived every day in the hope of finding the missing piece of the jigsaw and while Sam kept well it was relatively easy to carry on. After Sam passed away, a friend wrote to me and said that because of his attitude to his illness, Sam was never a child dying of leukaemia but just a child living each day happy to be well. I hope that was true.

CHAPTER 20

Once again we were adrift and once again a little bit of hope landed on our doorstep – an appointment with Matthew Manning whose waiting list we were on had become available. We drove up to East Anglia for our appointment and waited nervously for our turn to be seen. The healer had a very simple way of giving healing and, much to Sam's relief, didn't ask emotional questions! Sam sat in a simple chair and the healer sat with his hands lightly touching him for about thirty minutes. One of the unusual things about the appointment was the music that was being played. It was extremely loud! Sam felt very hot after the healing and we booked in for a treatment once a month. After the first treatment there was a decrease in the leukaemia cells and we were ecstatic, thinking this was the vital piece of the jigsaw we had been looking for. As time went on the disease began to increase once again but the initial positive result kept our hopes and therefore our spirits up.

We also had an appointment booked to see Charles Siddle in the New Year – I didn't believe we could see too many healers – but I received a telephone call saying Charles was very ill. I wondered who healed the healer? I decided to put my fear of rejection to one side and contact him to offer some healing. Charles did not want to see me or anybody else, as he was very ill with infected colitis. But when I rang he had just fallen over in the kitchen and, possibly in his desperation, he said that I could come and see him. He was obviously in a very low state and sounded tearful. When I arrived he looked terribly ill; he had burned himself when he fell and was in a dreadful state. He looked like a small, frightened animal and I tried to help as best as I could. I had worked with the elderly in the past and when I reassured him that I was not embarrassed by anything I was seeing, the fight seemed to go out of him, and he collapsed into a chair and allowed me to help.

Charles later credited me with saving his life. I do not think for a moment that I did; I simply cared for him as I would anyone who was ill. Unbeknown to me it was to be the beginning of an interesting and challenging relationship for both of us. Over the following weeks I talked to him on the telephone and visited him to give healing once or twice a week. Sam thought that his healer having healing from his mummy was all very amusing! A few weeks later Charles was admitted into hospital for an operation from which he recovered very quickly. Healing is a very good post-operative tool and in just a few weeks Charles was back on his feet again, remarkable for a man aged 73.

As Charles began to get well we talked more about healing matters and he suggested I might be interested in healing animals as well as people. I replied that I had no time at present to do this but when Sam was well again I might consider it. He was obviously reluctant for us to go our separate ways and persuaded me that by working alongside him a couple of days a week it would benefit Sam as well as me. Charles thought I spent too much time with Sam and by me being elsewhere David would have to be more involved in Sam's care, which would be good for all of us.

In the subsequent months I worked with Charles at the various clinics he held around the country – this was mostly at weekends when David was at home to look after the boys. We travelled many miles to the different clinics to heal animals and people so we had plenty of time to talk. I grew to know Charles very well during those journeys. He believed that his success as a healer was due to an old friend of his called Buster Lloyd Jones. Buster had been a well-known vet when he was alive and Charles believed that Buster was channelling his special healing powers through him.

Certainly Charles was an amazing animal healer, as well as being very good with backs and bones. He took to dropping into our house regularly and became a common sight at the door, saying he had received a message from Buster that Sam needed some more healing. We began giving healing to Sam together – Charles felt it would increase the amount of energy Sam would receive.

Sam seemed to like the thought that I was helping the animals and when I was away for the day he, David and Nick had quality 'boy time' together, playing endless computer games and eating junk food in front of the TV. In hindsight I think it was preparation for the time to come; I felt bereft when I first went away for the day but it was obvious that the boys were fine without me and I was learning a lot from Charles about animal healing. Eventually we found that we worked so well together that we decided to make our relationship more formal by going into business together. Our business was called The Beacon of Healing Light and is the sole trader name that I still use today for my private practice.

The months rolled on. The more Sam's marrow struggled with the leukaemia that was trying to take over, the more blood products Sam needed. Sam was now receiving three units of blood a week, which meant more trips to our local hospital for blood transfusions.

Sam was well known at the local hospital; I have very happy memories of him running up the corridor shouting, 'Come on, Mum, run!' as we went in for his transfusions. Even with a very low blood count he had the most extraordinary energy – I don't think anyone who saw us running into and out of the wards could quite believe that Sam was as ill as the tests said he was.

It was April 1998 and we were approaching the boys' birthdays. Nick would be fifteen and Sam would be ten. We had planned the birthday celebrations and were all looking forward to a weekend of fun. Sam had several friends around for a bowling party and he was, of course, the star of the show. It was very poignant looking at him with all his peers and not knowing what the future held for him. The monthly trips to the healer in Suffolk continued and I was giving Sam healing whenever he asked for it.

This would usually be if he felt his legs were a little less strong than he wanted them to be. Sam was a very keen footballer and loved playing football in our large garden with his friends. Such was

Sam's energy that he was playing football right up to the weekend before he died. For me this is one of the wonders of healing, to be able to offer quality of life, which for Sam meant having enough energy to play with his friends and to be able to live at home with his family. I wanted so much more than that for Sam, but we had a lot to be grateful for.

Shortly after the boys' birthdays, with very bad luck Sam had some bacteria travel up his Hickman line, infecting the line itself. Sam went into toxic shock and I rushed him over to our local hospital. The consultant told me to prepare for the worst as the last child to come in with this problem had been rushed into intensive care within hours. Sam was certainly very ill. He lay in bed saying nothing and I lay beside him giving healing, shouting in my mind at God (if he existed). Why was this happening? I couldn't stand to watch Sam suffer and felt at the time that, if he was going to die, it was best that he die then to stop him suffering.

Miraculously Sam started to improve within a few hours and I took him home that night. The doctors said we should stay but Sam wanted to go home and, given my belief that Sam's quality of life was paramount, I told the consultant that I would discharge Sam if necessary. He let us go and wished us well.

CHAPTER 21

Once again, it was as if a secret signal had gone off somewhere in the universe. A letter arrived from America; it was from Leonora Van Gills, a woman we had met the previous year, who had been introduced to us by Ashley's mother Lyn.

Leonora was now working for the Human Dolphin Institute in America and she had sent us the brochure about the work the institute were doing with sick children. One of the children featured in the brochure was a young girl who had been suffering from Acute Myeloid Leukaemia. The article was very inspiring and after reading it Sam and I looked at each other and laughed – we both knew that very soon we would be swimming with the dolphins.

It seemed impossible to contemplate how we would manage it as Sam was very weak after his line infection and the expense was beyond us as a family, but somehow I knew that we would go. We began to read all we could about dolphins, watching videos borrowed from the library about their wonderful healing power. David's large extended family became aware of what we wanted to do and very kindly clubbed together and gave us some money, making it possible for all four of us to go to America.

Money was only part of the problem. Sam would be having to get in the water with the dolphins and his Hickman line was going to make that difficult. The staff at Great Ormond Street really were an enormous help. They arranged special dressings that would make swimming possible and provided me with a suitcase full of all the medication I could possibly need. I could not have wished for more support from them.

All that remained was to get Sam strong enough to make the flight. The institute was in the Gulf of Mexico so we would have to fly to Florida and then hire a car for the long journey to Panama City. I don't think anyone thought Sam would be well enough to go but on 26 June we flew out to Florida. Some friends had rung Virgin to ask if an upgrade was possible for us. We flew Upper Class with Virgin Airlines, the second time Virgin had helped Sam. Sam and Nick were thrilled, and Sam laid back in his huge seat and called for the hostess to bring him another orange juice! It was a magic moment.

We arrived in Florida to the 'worst bush fires that had occurred for many years'. A sign in the hotel foyer warned that anyone with health problems should stay indoors. Luckily we were leaving the next day to drive up to the Gulf of Mexico, so it wasn't going to be a problem for us.

The magic of the Human Dolphin Institute was that the dolphins we were to swim with were wild. This meant that each day we would go out on a small boat and hope to have our encounter with these beautiful untamed creatures.

On our first day out on the sea we saw a mother and her young pup. It was an emotional moment and the symbolism of mother and child moved me to tears. They swam alongside the boat as if accompanying us out to sea. We had several sightings that day but did not have the opportunity to put Sam in the sea with them. We arrived home tired and hungry, our appetites whetted for our anticipated encounter, looking forward to the next day when we hoped for better luck. I slept badly that night. We had come all this way – what if we didn't manage to swim with the dolphins?

The next day we were out on the sea for hours. Nick began to feel seasick – I felt so sorry for him and began to wonder if it was all for nothing, this struggle to come out here to swim with dolphins that were nowhere to be seen. Leonora and her partner said that we should moor the boat and have some lunch; I could see by Sam's face that he had lost interest and wanted to go back to the shore. We needed some help.

In my mind I asked my mum for a bit of help and at that moment a large rainbow appeared in the sky. I pointed it out to Leonora and she said, 'Where there are rainbows, there are dolphins.' As she spoke I heard Sam shouting behind me, 'Dolphins!' There were at least ten dolphins surrounding our boat. Leonora and her partner leaped into action and within minutes we had set off again following the dolphins.

Eventually the dolphins stopped and Sam was lowered onto the back of the small inflatable that they had brought especially for this trip. It would allow Sam to get as close as possible to the dolphins before being put in the water. The dolphins circled the boat and then swam right up to him where he sat in the small inflatable. As they did so they turned on their sides to work their magic, making the amazing clicking noise we had heard on the videos we had watched back home in England. They made the most wonderful sight, ducking and diving. They seemed to be smiling and laughing with their happy faces, which were reflected in Sam's smiling, happy face as he splashed the water next to them. The encounter went on for about fifteen minutes and then the dolphins left us. Many people have talked of the effect of looking into the eye of a wild dolphin – for me it was the most incredible moment, a connection that was beyond words and made the tears stream down my face. Nick felt the same; in fact, I think everyone on the boat was crying at that moment.

The effect on Sam was instantaneous – it was if he had overdosed on sugar and was in the middle of a high! He turned into a clown for the return journey.

We have some video footage of him that day that I will always treasure. I knew in my heart that, whatever happened, from that moment onwards the trip had been worthwhile for the effect it had on him. Over the following nights I had several very strange dreams, some of which involved seeing Sam in the middle of a bright blue light. The dreams always ended the same way, with me being jolted awake in tears. I had no idea what the dreams meant but I hoped that the blue light meant that someone was sending Sam healing. One of the dreams featured Princess Diana, who had died the previous year. I saw Sam and her together in a bright blue light and again awoke very upset – I did not want to see my son with someone who was in spirit, I wanted Sam here with me.

We left Panama beach the next day and returned to Florida for the rest of our holiday. It was a surreal experience, pretending everything was normal. We were acting just like all the other families having a good time, but we were not normal and the constant reality of our desperate situation was very difficult to deal with in this adventure playground for children and adults alike. Sam had one infusion of blood while we were in America but he remained well for the whole trip. I was not sorry to leave America; we had achieved our goal of swimming with the dolphins and now I just wanted to go home.

CHAPTER 22

We arrived back in England and almost the first thing we did was to pick Zack up from the kennels. Sam was really happy to be back. He seemed different in some way but I could not put my finger on how. After a few weeks of being at home Sam developed a chest infection (a very common problem after a long flight), so the hospital took blood cultures and I was instructed to start routine antibiotics. On 3 August Sam was well enough to play in the garden with Nick and then the next day he became very sleepy and we spent the day cuddled up on the sofa.

As the day went on I began to feel tearful and worried and when David arrived home from work I was very relieved to see him. Sam woke up and chatted to him and seemed to be feeling a little better, so I went off to work on the computer in the other room. I had agreed to work on a book about Charles Siddle's life and now that David was home I worked at the computer for a few hours to steady myself.

Sam walked into the room and sat down behind me. He said, 'Come on, Mum, I'd like to have a bath now.' When I turned around to look at him his eyes had changed colour, they were the most amazing china blue, not Sam's eyes at all. I jumped up and held him and for a moment he stopped breathing, I thought he had gone there and then. As I held him he started to breath again and amazingly we went off upstairs for a bath.

It was the first time in the whole three years that I had had the thought, but I knew in that moment that we would lose Sam that night. I put him in the bath and we had our usual chats and then went back downstairs. I think in hindsight I was calm because I was in shock – I just carried on normally so as not to alarm or frighten him. I told David what I felt and he looked at me in disbelief. I went upstairs and spoke to Nick to try and prepare him; he looked at me blankly and said not to be so stupid, how could Sam be dying when he was downstairs watching TV. Which was, I guess, logical to him.

When I returned downstairs David was in shock in the kitchen and Sam was watching TV with Nick. I was very calm; the only thing that mattered to me was Sam, and I cuddled up on the sofa with him. Nick went off to bed and again I tried to talk to him about what I felt was going to happen that night, but it was too painful and I left Nick in David's care, returning downstairs to Sam.

Some time later Sam pushed me away and said he wanted me to sit on another chair. I believe he couldn't let go when I was so close to him as the pull of my love to keep him there was so strong. He must have known this on some subconscious level and pushed me away. At about 2 a.m. (I had drifted off to sleep where I was sitting), I was brought awake by a change in Sam's breathing. I leaped to my feet and woke David, who was sitting next to Sam. We both held him and cried quietly as his breathing slowed and eventually stopped with a last sigh. I spoke to Sam as he slipped peacefully away and told him to go towards the light where Nanny would be waiting for him. I could hardly breathe and wanted desperately to die too. Our world had come to an end.

David and I sat and held Sam until eventually I said that I wanted to dress him in some warm clothes. It didn't make sense, but my mother's instinct wanted to wrap him up for his journey. While David rang for the doctor I dressed Sam in his favourite outfit: tracksuit bottoms and bright T-shirt with a bright-red, hooded fleecy top. I also put a warm pair of socks on.

The doctor arrived and asked some questions. I'd never seen her before and I thought she considered this to be a sudden death. I'm afraid I was a bit short with her and while I was telling her not to be so stupid Sam's mouth turned up at the corners. It was an amazing moment, as if he was still there and laughing at me for giving the doctor a hard time. We kept Sam with us until the morning and Nick came downstairs and spent some time with us all. It was important to me to keep Sam in the house until I was quite sure in my own mind that he had gone. The undertakers arrived about seven-thirty in the morning to take him to the chapel of rest.

David took care of all the practical details that day. I wasn't interested in doing anything; my darling Sam was gone and nothing else mattered to me. I'm sure in hindsight we were all in shock. Sam had been ill for so long that none of us ever really expected him to die. Despite his medical prognosis it seemed he would live forever. Dying so suddenly was very much Sam's style – he was always full of surprises and I would rather it happened the way it did than have him linger on for months. We all dealt with the horror of that first day without Sam in our own way.

Nick stayed in his room, not wishing to come down into the room where Sam had died. Eventually he did come down but we didn't discuss anything of the previous night's events. It wasn't until months later that he was ready to talk to me about how he felt. For now we all kept our thoughts and feelings to ourselves, acting on autopilot.

Later that day Charles Siddle called. He had received a call from a family who wanted us to go to Cambridge to see a child who was dying of leukaemia. He thought I wouldn't want to go, but I did. Sam didn't need me now, but if I could be of help to someone else I would do what I could. I also felt that it would in some small way take my mind off what was I was trying to deal with at home. Charles, Nick and I drove up to Cambridge in silence and as we approached the house we could see weeping people leaving. Nick stayed in the car (he had agreed to come with us as I refused to leave him alone at home while David was in town dealing with the official paperwork about Sam's death).

I could see that we were too late but knocked on the door anyway. The father answered and I asked whether he still wanted us to come in. We were led into the lounge where the young boy lay. He was the same age as Sam but had gone completely yellow, as his liver had failed. I knew there was no point in giving him healing; he was beyond that. I spoke to the parents saying how sorry I was and that I understood their pain. They didn't believe that I could possibly understand their pain until I explained briefly that I had just lost a child, and then they looked at me in disbelief and we all cried together. I know that Charles and I helped those parents that day as we talked about the two children we had just lost and our belief that they were safe in spirit.

I believe that journey was a spiritual test. If I had refused to help because of my own grief I might as well have given up any thoughts of healing there and then. What was it to be?

The next week passed in a blur. Because the end had been so swift it was a shock to everybody and many people were deeply upset. Sam was buried the following week in our local churchyard. It was a lovely sunny day for a lovely sunny child and I wore a bright summer's frock, as Sam would have wanted. I have no doubt that I was helped that day by spirit and by Sam, as I felt completely composed as people wept around me. When Sam's coffin was lowered into the ground a shaft of sunshine lit up the spot. David and I felt totally numb, while Nick had chosen to take Zack, Sam's dog, for a walk in a nearby field while the burial service was carried out.

When everyone had gone home and Nick was asleep I climbed into Sam's bed. I moved into Sam's room that day. I felt closest to him there and got some comfort from sleeping in the sheets that he had slept in. Over the following days all the medical equipment was taken away and all medications were returned to the hospital.

I began to feel that only the knowledge that Sam was safe in spirit would help me get through this time, and to get that knowledge I had to find a good medium, someone who could prove to me that there is a life beyond this life, and that somehow I could communicate with my beloved Sam. I know that this is a common reaction for people who have lost loved ones and I find it completely understandable – until you can come to terms with thinking of your loved one in whatever place they have gone to, it is very hard to get on with your life.

They were desperate days. My faith had completely deserted me, and I kept thinking that Sam was now just bones in the ground. All of my previous beliefs about the spirit world existing as a different vibration, with our loved ones being together, became unbelievable and I became lost in my grief and despair. I took care of Nick as best I could but we all fumbled our way through that terrible time. Nick didn't want to talk about Sam and neither David or myself had anything to say to each other. We were all lost for words. I spent a lot of time sitting by Sam's grave; I talked to Sam, begging him to give me a sign that he was safe.

The place where Sam is buried is a beautiful country graveyard with many travellers' graves; right next to Sam was the grave of a small child who had died at the age of two. The travellers who visited the grave were very good to me, explaining how to take care of the new grave by putting a groundsheet down and making me a makeshift cross to put Sam's name on. Neither David nor Nick could bear to be there but I felt closest to Sam when I sat next to the grave. Benny, the head traveller, had apparently had quite a colourful past but I can only speak well of him and his family as they supported me through those first few months.

The travellers always seemed to be there and at the beginning I found it very irritating; I wanted to be alone to weep and wail. Because there was always someone there I didn't have the opportunity to wallow in my grief, and in hindsight this was a very good thing for me. I had, after all, told many patients over the years that their loved ones were not lost to them, merely in a different place. Gradually I began to realise that now it was my turn to 'walk the walk' and not just 'talk the talk'.

CHAPTER 23

My experience with mediums had not been that good in the past. When Mum had passed into spirit I attended a local spiritualist church a few times, hoping that I would receive a message from her. I felt that if she could have spoken to me she would have, and I came away disappointed.

I had continued to believe there was a spirit world to which my mum and now Sam had gone, but I was feeling that my whole belief system was on the line. I did believe that Sam was safe, free and healthy again in spirit, but my belief system had been shaken and, like many people, I needed proof of that to fully regain my faith. I needed to know that Sam was well and happy and not missing us. I asked around and was given the name of a medium who lived locally.

David did not want to come with me to the medium and I went along to my appointment (ten days after Sam had died) thinking to myself that I had to receive proof that day. Our bond had been so strong that if Sam could talk to me he would, and if I received nothing, then in my mind there was no longer any point in going on, as all that I believed in would become a lot of misguided nonsense.

In my mind I felt that Nick would be fine with David, and I could go and be with Sam; this was totally wrong, of course. It would have been a terrible thing to have done to Nick, but grief can make you very selfish and at that time it seemed a rational idea to me.

I knocked at the door of what seemed like a very ordinary house, and was greeted by a kindly looking woman. She introduced herself as Gill, the medium's wife. I waited for my appointment and was eventually led into a room where Ron Moulding, the medium, sat quietly in a comfortable chair. He wasn't what I expected, just a kind-looking man, very much like a lot of other normal, middle-aged men, with nothing strange or mystic looking about him at all. Ron asked me if I knew what he did and I said I did. He then asked me who I wanted to speak to. This was an unexpected bonus; so many mediums will bring you Aunt Nelly or Uncle Reg who you have no real connection with, but here I was being asked, 'Who do you want to speak to?' I replied straight away, Sam. I gave him no clues who Sam was, nor did he ask for any, I simply gave his name.

Ron's style of reading is unique. He began to talk rapidly. There was no opportunity for me to do anything other than listen. The reading was taped, which was just as well as I was soon in floods of tears as he began to give me the most incredible proof that Sam was indeed safe and in spirit with his nanny. Ron told me things he could not possibly have known, such as how old Sam was, what disease he had and how many times he had lost his hair. He also gave me very detailed descriptions of the treatments Sam had undergone, trips that we had been on and, of vital importance to me, where he was buried and details of items I had placed in his coffin. David had also apparently put a ring and a letter in the coffin for Sam that I had not known about – no one but Sam would have known about those things.

Ron also said that the night Sam had passed he had almost died several hours before (this would be when I noticed the change in the colour of his eyes) and that I had said, 'Go to the light, Sam.' The tape was about thirty minutes long and was packed with information that convinced me that Sam was where I hoped he would be. Ron had never met me before and knew nothing about our family, but the gift he gave me that day was immeasurable and I will always treasure the tape that I received.

Not everyone believes in mediums and many are, I'm sure, not bona fide. However, as I found, visiting a medium can help with private grief. If any of my private patients need this kind of help, however, I will only ever recommend Ron. I'm sure that there are other good mediums around, but Ron's gift of being able to communicate with the one you need to speak to is quite remarkable and, for me at least, truly a life-saver.

Having the evidence I needed was wonderful, but of course it did not change the fact that Sam was gone in the physical sense of the word. Yes, I now knew he was safe, but the pain of losing him was beyond any words I could write. It wasn't just my pain of course; Nick retreated into a place where I couldn't reach him. I knew that all I could do was to be there and take care of his physical needs. I hoped that later he would have some healing from me that would help him release the emotional pain he was hiding, but I knew it would be when he was ready and on his terms.

David, of course, was hurting badly, no doubt made worse by the fact that our marriage was on the rocks. I think that the best way to describe those next few months was that we each survived in our own way. We did not grieve together, but maybe that is impossible, as each family member has a different relationship with the one who has gone, therefore the feelings and the pain are different for everyone.

My way of coping was to throw myself into my work. Healing was helping to fill the void left by Sam. It didn't change anything, of course. At the end of a long day's healing with Charles, I would spend time with Nick and then lock myself away and cry bitterly looking for some answers, finding nothing except more tears.

Charles and I were working together almost every day now, travelling miles to heal animals and people in the clinics that he held around the country; we also worked together from my healing room built specially within our house. Building work on the healing room for my now-thriving private practice had begun before Sam had passed away and David had encouraged the idea, thinking it would help me in some way if I kept busy.

People began to arrive for healing with many different types of problems: stress-related illnesses such as irritable bowel syndrome (IBS), bowel disorders of all kinds, migraines, back problems, immune problems, almost every kind of illness came through our healing room and we were very busy. We also began to see a lot of people with cancer, and I was reminded again of the role healing can play in the fight against this dreadful disease. It seemed that whenever I saw someone with cancer I heard Sam whispering in my ear, 'Don't forget the children, Mummy.' I vowed to try and find a way that I could help children and people who were sick in hospital.

If you are well enough to be an out-patient there isn't really a problem in accessing a healer, but if you are an in-patient it is much harder. I wanted to try and change this. I wanted to try and talk to the doctors I knew at Great Ormond Street to try and persuade them that it wasn't just Sam who could benefit from healing, but their other patients could too.

CHAPTER 24

For almost a year, I worked hard with Charles but felt dead inside. I would often think about Great Ormond Street and wonder how I could approach the hospital to try and get the doctors to listen to me. I wanted them to hear about the role healing could play alongside their conventional treatments. What would be the most effective way to approach the hospital? I knew that any presentation I offered to make at that time would probably be seen by them as a mother working through her grief, and I wanted to be taken seriously and not be dismissed in this way. As yet I did not know how best to do this, so I waited and waited until I could come up with a better way of getting them to accept what I had to say.

Charles and I presented a workshop at the Mind, Body and Spirit Festival in London about the work we did with animals and people; we were happy to talk about healing whenever we were given the opportunity. We looked an unlikely pair, but the message we carried was the same – healing was a wonderful tool whatever your problem in life. At the festival we met up with Denise Linn (a well-known healer from America) and I thanked her for the absent healing she had been sending to Sam.

I had asked her to send healing when we had met her at the previous year's festival. During Sam's illness I had written to her occasionally to update her on his progress. A few weeks after I had told her that Sam was no longer in need of her healing, I received a package through the post. It was from Denise and she had put together several items to celebrate Sam's life. I was so touched that she had taken the time to do that; I decided that if I ever became well known for my work as a healer I would try and emulate her and the love she sent out to everyone who asked for help.

I arranged a lot of absent healing for Sam when he was first diagnosed; it was really helpful and I often use this technique myself if a request for my healing has come from an area of the country (or indeed a different country) that makes it difficult for the patient to get to my healing room.

My first experience of absent healing was while working on animals with Charles Siddle. Charles had taught me how to send absent healing, saying that it could be a very useful tool, especially if we were unable to visit an animal for some time. His experience was that absent healing was very effective and he had achieved very good results with the technique.

I used to suffer badly with migraines and on one particular occasion I was speaking to Charles on the telephone when I began to experience blurred vision, one of the first warning signs of a migraine approaching. Charles told me to go and sit quietly and he would send me some healing for the migraine. I hung up the telephone and sat down in chair, thinking to myself that this wasn't going to work – my migraines needed medication! As I was sitting there wondering what I could do to keep the migraine at bay and what tablets I had in the house, I was suddenly hit by a bolt of energy running through my body. I sat there wondering what on earth was happening. Then I remembered that Charles had said he would send me healing. I can only say that I definitely felt the energy, even though I did not at the time believe that I would; also, the migraine completely disappeared. While I had arranged absent healing for Sam many times I had never received it personally before or felt the energy in such a tangible way.

After that experience I began to take the absent healing seriously, beginning to get very good results with it, especially on animals. One of the first success stories that I can recall began with a call from a lady with a sick cat. The cat had been diagnosed by the vet as having acute kidney problems. I spoke to the owner and decided to send absent healing as she and the cat were in Wales, which meant I would be unable to visit for some time. We arranged a time for later on that day when I would send healing to the cat, and the owner rang me excitedly the next day to tell me that, at the exact time I was sending healing, the cat got up from where it was lying, went over to its drinking bowl and took its first drink of water for many hours. Happily the cat went on to live for a further two years before passing away. The cat was already elderly but still the healing had enabled it to have an extra year or two with its owner. Often when the animal is so well loved, the extra time healing can bring about is a priceless gift to the owner.

Another example of successful absent healing was with a horse that was suffering an acute episode of colic. Colic is an extremely painful spasm in the gut and in extreme cases the horse may have to be put down. The owner had rung me in great distress; the vet was with the horse and was very concerned. The horse had a history of colic problems and I immediately sent the healing while the vet was in the stable with the horse. Much to the vet's amazement the horse began to breathe more easily and its heartbeat began to stabilise as the pain from the colic spasms abated. When I arrived at the stables the horse was back to its normal self and the vet was looking very puzzled. It matters not to me that the vet didn't understand the process of healing; the only thing that mattered is that the horse was well and happy and moving freely about its stable.

There are many examples of absent healing working successfully, not just on animals, but on people and situations. One I particularly remember was a young man whom I had first met once I had begun working at the hospital. When I met Patrick he was in the last stages of his life, having been given the news that there was nothing more medically to offer him. It was arranged that he would be transferred back to his home town on the south coast where he was expected to pass away within days. In his last week at the hospital in London he received several healing treatments, and each treatment was a very profound spiritual experience for him and for me. He always saw what he described as the brightest light imaginable, in which he saw faces and shapes, and after the treatment was completed we would sit and discuss his experiences. The sessions left him feeling supported, uplifted and, importantly for him, able to communicate with his family about how he felt about dying.

When Patrick was transferred to his local hospital, his mother rang me regularly to update me and to ask for healing to be sent to her son. I eventually received a call from her saying that she felt Patrick had taken a turn for the worse and she tearfully asked me to send healing to help him stay for a little while longer. I knew how that mother felt – I would have done anything to have gained an extra day with Sam if I could have done. I gently explained to her that I could not direct the healing in that way but that I would send healing for Patrick's highest good and if that meant that he was able to stay for a little longer, so be it.

When I heard from her the following day I fully expected her to say Patrick had passed, however there was a lightness in her voice that suggested otherwise. She explained that when I had sent the healing, Patrick had roused from his sleep and asked for pizza and chips to be brought to him! No one could quite believe what was happening but he ate heartily and over the next week saw many friends to say his goodbyes. Finally, a week later, he passed away peacefully; he was obviously ready to leave and had completed all he had wanted to do. I like to think that in time, over the years, his mother will remember that last week, maybe even laugh at the memory of Patrick sitting up in his supposed deathbed, eating pizza and chips. I will certainly never forget him.

Often I will be asked to send healing to a situation, a son or daughter perhaps who is very stressed at sitting an exam. Whether it is a placebo effect or not I don't know, but it is remarkably effective for pre-exam nerves, fear of flying or even driving tests.

I prepare myself for absent healing by sitting in my healing room in an upright chair that I use for meditating. I find the breath is a very important tool for me in achieving a sense of attunement with the healing energy – breath is the means by which I connect to that energy. I begin to breathe in deeply through my nose and exhale forcefully through my mouth (some people may experience a feeling of light-headedness, but resumption of normal breathing should settle you down). By breathing in this way my mind and body become still and I am ready to begin the session of absent healing.

Firstly, I bring to my mind a mental picture of the person or animal that requires healing, and mentally surround them with light – the light is usually bright white but can change with each person that I bring into my thoughts. If I am aware of a particular problem I will visualise the problem area being bathed in light and, in the case of tumours, see them dissolving away. When I am finished, I will break my thoughts away and mentally surround the object with light once again (enclosing them in a circle of light) and then separate my thoughts from them before moving on to the next person/animal/situation on my list. When I have finished the absent healing session I will once again focus my attentions on my own breathing – breathing deeply through my nose and out through my mouth while pushing my feet firmly against the floor to ground myself. I mentally surround myself with healing light and then take a long drink of water. I am then ready to get on with normal life.

My hands become very hot during the healing, which is quite normal. I usually like to keep a record of my absent healing and encourage feedback from people who have requested it. This way I can evaluate my progress and my healing abilities.

In my absent-healing book at home in my healing room are all the names of people who have requested absent healing. One of these names is Eve. I have only seen Eve once for a session in my healing room. Distance and circumstances have made it impossible to see her and so she requested that I send her absent healing. Eve is fighting throat and mouth cancer and so far has outlived all the doctors' expectations. She is a very strong person mentally and the way she is living her life, despite her incredibly difficult situation, is an inspiration to all who meet her. Eve has her own very special gift – she has the ability to tune into our loved ones who have passed into spirit, and then writes poetry with the messages she receives. She recently sent me a poem that she had written about my son Sam and with her permission I have pleasure in printing it here for all to share.

To My Dearest Mother

I am not alone, do rest assured,
Love is everywhere through this open door.
I am your golden boy, full of glee,
As you would wish, upon your knee.

My eyes are bright, I have no pain,
My smile comes all the way to reign.
I am so close and feel your heart,
Remember mother we are not apart.

Your gift of healing is all around,
Helping those with love and sound,
To be at peace from earthly pain,
The world has everything to gain.

I am Sam, your boy, cheeky and proud
To have such a loving mother around.
Channelling energy to all who wish,
Healing and loving, dear Mum I kiss.

Ruth Evelyn

As I said, I have only met Eve once so the detail in this poem is very good. Sam's smile was a joy to behold, and the reference to healing with sound is, I think, because I always use music when I am healing. All in all I accept this poem as a link with Sam and know yet again that he is happy and free in spirit, free to come and go as he wishes, which is what I wish for him.

CHAPTER 25

David and I were living separate lives by now and I began to talk to him about separating. He would have none of it and I put the idea to one side. However, I had long conversations with Nick about the possibility of David and me living apart, trying to prepare him for what I saw as the inevitable. Nick responded to the news with his usual pragmatism. For him it would be nothing compared to the death of Sam and he felt that, as the atmosphere in the house was so bad, things might even improve. While I was shocked that he was so aware of the problems between the two of us (I had thought that we were managing to hide things from him) I was relieved that he viewed things in a similar way to me – that this next stage of our lives was going to be less difficult than we had experienced with the loss of Sam. Who knows how long we might have all gone on living like this, but something happened that changed everything.

I had arranged to do a sponsored skydive for the Anthony Nolan Bone Marrow Charity. Before the jump we were taken through the safety procedures by the expert staff at the centre in Peterborough, where we were taught how to exit the aircraft and land correctly. Everybody else was very nervous; some people were even being sick with fear. I felt nothing. When I jumped out of the aeroplane I couldn't have cared whether I lived or died. When I landed on the ground everyone else was elated, but again I felt nothing. Later that day I played back the video recording of the jump, and as I watched myself jumping out of the aircraft's door I was shocked by the lack of emotion on my face. I looked as if I was walking into a supermarket, not jumping out of an aircraft and I felt for the first time very, very sad. It was obvious when I looked at the film that I was not alive at all. Yes I was breathing, I was walking, I was even jumping out of an aircraft but I might as well have been dead as my face showed that there were no feelings there at all. It was then that I decided that, since I was still alive, I might as well engage in life. That meant starting to feel again, good feelings as well as bad. The way I was living at present was not really living at all; I was just going through the motions.

The following day I filed for divorce – I knew that David had been short-changed as I didn't have any feelings left for him any more. I cared about him, but not in the way that two people living together should. He deserved more than that after all he had been through and I wanted to be free to lead my own life, as I should have done before.

Life began to get better from then on. I talked to Nick about the divorce and, while he was not happy at all the changes it would involve, he said he would cope.

It was around this time that I read an article in the *Daily Mail* about a little girl who had recently died of leukaemia at Great Ormond Street Hospital. Her mother had written a very moving article about her child, but what struck me about the story was that it seemed that the little girl had not enjoyed the quality of life that Sam had. Given our experience with Sam's illness, I felt strongly that it didn't have to be that way as there are many other things that can help. I rang the *Express* newspaper, who were happy to write an article about healing and the possible role it may have alongside conventional medicine.

The response to the article was overwhelming. So many parents contacted me to say that they also believed that healing should be available in hospitals that it finally gave me the motivation and ammunition to approach hospitals to put the case for healing to be made available alongside conventional medicine.

I approached Great Ormond Street Hospital and I was invited to talk to the doctors about the role healing could play there. I remember the day very well. It was the first day I had been back to the hospital since Sam had died and I visited the beautiful little chapel that they have there, hoping for some inspiration and to calm myself. I asked Sam to come in and sit on my shoulder and help me to find the right words that would open these doctors' minds to the help that healing could give their little patients.

The talk took place in a large auditorium and I was introduced by Paul Veys, Sam's consultant. I looked out at the doctors and nurses who had come along to hear me talk and again asked Sam to help me. I spoke about Sam's journey within their hospital and the quality of life he had enjoyed, giving them examples of how healing may be of benefit not only to their patients, but also the children's families and the staff on the wards. They were very attentive and I felt that it had gone well, but for the moment their doors remain closed to healers being part of the care they offer. In hindsight I can see that they may have thought I was validating Sam's death by approaching them about healing in this way, but I was not. I knew what healing could do for the children and I wanted to be given an opportunity to show the staff that healing was not just effective for Sam but could be just as valuable for others in his position.

I had been thinking about this for so long and believed so passionately that healing would help in-patients in hospitals that I was not to be thwarted so easily. I approached University College London Hospital (UCLH), since I knew that Stephen Rowley, who had nursed Sam at Great Ormond Street some years ago, was working there. I rang him and asked whether there would be any interest in healing on the haematology ward. The good news was that Stephen told me that they did have a complementary team as part of the unit but, as yet, no healer. The complementary team at that time had a counsellor, a reflexologist/aromatherapist and a newly appointed hypnotherapist.

Stephen said that he would arrange an appointment for me to speak to the ward manager, but he knew that the manager was very sceptical of healing and advised me not to be too hopeful. I went along to my meeting with Tim Jackson in June 1999. I explained to Tim all the positive things that healing could do on his ward and waited for him to say thanks, but no thanks.

He didn't. What he did say, however, was that it was all very interesting but that he couldn't afford to pay me. Excitedly I said that payment wasn't a problem, that I only wanted to be given the opportunity to prove a need, at least to start with. I was fortunate to be able to agree to his offer of unpaid work as my private work as a healer and my work with Charles was going well and I could therefore afford to offer the hospital one day a week.

I was also still married and as such didn't have to worry about a roof over my head just yet. I knew that in the future my finances would be a problem for me but at the time it was more important to me that I could offer the time to prove a need for healing. I was also confident that, given the opportunity, healing would be a success in this setting and then perhaps the hospital would be able to pay me as the other therapists were being paid.

A miracle was in progress. I was going to be allowed in to work one day a week. My first day of work was to be the following Friday, nearly a year to the day that Sam had passed into spirit. I took that as a positive sign.

I had mixed feelings that first day as I walked into UCLH in my professional (though unpaid) role of healer. It brought back memories; this was the hospital that we had brought Nick to for the cell collection that we had hoped would help Sam. That had been three years ago and travelling up in the lift was a very strange sensation but I was happy to be given this opportunity to show what healing could do in this acute-care setting. I had many advantages, as I knew only too well the procedures that are in place to protect the patients, who were immune-suppressed due to their treatments, and this stood me in good stead. There are strict protocols for entering a patient's room; cleanliness is vital in protecting the patients from infection and, of course, seeing patients looking very poorly with machines attached to them was a familiar sight for me.

I began my day by introducing myself to the patients – I knew that if I waited for referrals from the staff I would not be doing very much healing as the staff did not at this point know what I was offering. I explained to the patients what my role on the ward was, including how a treatment may be able to help them.

My description of healing today is exactly the same as when I explained it that first day at the hospital. I have found it essential to speak of healing in very down-to-earth language. Of course there is a much bigger picture than the one I paint, but patients in this setting only need a certain amount of information. They are having enough trouble trying to deal with their protocols and the names of drugs, without me giving them information that is over and above what they need to experience the benefit of healing.

I began by explaining that no matter what we may call healing (it is known by many names, including Reiki, spiritual healing and therapeutic touch), all healing methods have one thing in common and that is energy. I then explained that a healer believes that we have a physical body that is surrounded by several energy bodies. When we are ill, either physically, emotionally or mentally, these bodies can become unbalanced. A healer such as myself can give the patient more energy and help rebalance those energy bodies by laying hands gently on their body, beginning at their head and moving via a series of hand positions to their feet.

When I begin working back up the body I work some two to three inches *above* the body. I always explain I will be doing this, otherwise the patient may think I have finished the treatment. (Many times I have received healing and have been irritated that the healer did not tell me this – I felt I had to open my eyes to see where the healer was!) I work above the body on that second move up the body because the emotional energy body resonates slightly off the physical body. The energy is very potent and useful here, because a patient is very likely to be in a great deal of stress due to their medical situation. The shock of diagnosis and treatment will have been traumatic.

My belief is that everything we experience emotionally will be felt in our emotional energy body before it impacts on the physical body. Therefore the emotional body will need to be rebalanced as part of the healing process. When I have finished working above the body I return to a hands-on position on the patient's head to finish the treatment. When I am ready to end the session I give the patient a prearranged signal and gently rouse them. If the patient wants to, we will discuss how they felt during the treatment. Most people *do* want to talk about their session, as the physical sensations and visual experiences of receiving their first healing are often very profound.

I was run off my feet that first day; everybody I spoke to wanted to try the healing. Because the patients were so ill, the energy had a very profound effect on them and they loved it. Many of them couldn't wait to have more and were disappointed that it was only available once a week at present.

I made a point that day of also offering treatments to some of the staff. I believed that if they felt the healing energy it would have more impact than anything I could say to them. As well as helping those members of staff themselves (since they have very stressful jobs), they would then be better able to explain to patients what my service was and why it was available; they might even suggest patients seek some healing from me. Anything that helped patients become aware of how healing might help them was a benefit in my mind.

At the end of the day I drove home feeling absolutely shattered but with the wonderful glow that comes from doing a good job and making a difference to people's lives. I chatted away in my head to Sam, hoping that he was proud of me and of what I was doing. I had no doubt that Sam was sitting on my shoulder just as he had said he would, and whatever I achieved from this moment on would be because of him – it was his life's gift to me. I missed him more than ever but, like many people before and after me, I would have to learn to walk with that pain until we met again in spirit.

The next month passed very quickly and the healing proved itself, as I had known it would. Tim Jackson called me into his office and congratulated me on a job well done. He said that he was convinced of the benefits to his patients and we discussed a suitable rate of pay. I continued to work just the one day a week, but I was now a paid healer working within the NHS, an incredibly unusual state of affairs. Any patient has a right to ask for the services of a spiritual healer and I am aware that many healers have been invited into hospital by patients (as we did for Sam with Kim). There may be volunteer healers working within hospitals as well, but to be paid by the NHS as a healer is a unique position to be in.

My goal is that by publicising my work and its benefits I will not be in that unique position much longer and that more hospitals will open their doors to healers such as myself. The fact that at UCLH the complementary team are paid as therapists means that our trust is operating integrated care at its best, offering treatments to in-patients, out-patients, carers and staff. It was the start of an incredible journey working professionally within the state sector.

It is often very challenging to work on a hospital ward; if you are hoping to be warmly welcomed by the medical staff you will be sadly disappointed (they are far too busy to notice what individuals are doing). You just have to get on with your job and be content with the response from patients. The unit I work on is an acute-care ward, where the patients are actively fighting their illnesses, such as cancer; they are undergoing very strong treatments that can often be very hard to tolerate. Quite often the cancer or other illness will respond, but the patient will succumb to an infection caused by their lowered immune system.

As I had discovered, healing is a powerful tool in this setting, helping to take away pain, reducing side effects and, most beneficially, helping to create a positive attitude. It is well documented that a positive outlook can be helpful when fighting an illness such as cancer, but for some patients this is impossible to achieve by themselves. Healing can and does help enormously to achieve this positivity and, in turn, a better quality of life.

As a healer working within this setting I also found that I needed to have self-healing techniques. In the same way that the staff must find, no matter how professional you are, there are times when you will connect personally with a patient and the resulting emotions can be difficult to deal with (another reason why I was so keen to offer my services to staff if they wanted them).

It was to help myself deal with this load that led me to learn about Reiki. One of the differences in the teaching of Reiki and spiritual healing is that with Reiki you are shown how to give yourself a treatment. Sam had given me a book about Reiki years previously, and I had read with interest that Reiki could be a useful self-development and self-healing tool. I thought that it could be of use to me now as it was not always easy to find the time to see a healer myself.

'Hands-on healing' can be called many things – it seems that you only have to pick up the latest newspaper or magazine to read yet another article featuring a supposedly new therapy that, to my mind, is simply another commercial way of marketing what is essentially healing. The roots of Reiki are well written about and I will offer only a brief insight into the basis of the Reiki healing system (some further sources are given at the end of the book).

The traditional Reiki story begins in the 1800s in Japan, but many believe Reiki had been around for a long time even before then. Teaching methods and techniques have undergone changes and many different branches have evolved. Each of these branches claims to be the only way to use Reiki. This is nonsense. Whatever you call Reiki you are simply channelling energy, which will help the patient in whatever way is needed most. Traditional *Usui* Reiki is probably the closest to the original brought from Japan. It teaches Reiki in three degrees: Reiki 1, Reiki 2 and Master/Teacher's level.

Level 1 is to open you to receive energy by creating a pure channel, which opens from the crown chakra through the brow, heart, solar plexus, and back out through the hands – I will describe chakras in more detail in the next chapter. This process is achieved by the Reiki master/teacher, who ideally should have been attuned to the *Usui* system and obtained many years of experience. The channel that has been created means that the energy will flow through you, not from you.

It is for you to practise on yourself, friends, family, pets, etc. (with the help of the manual that you will be given as part of your Reiki training), but most importantly this tool could be the start of you taking charge of your own life. Reiki can help you to change your life patterns, and this self-healing process will often start after you have been attuned to Reiki 1. It is not uncommon for people to experience emotional and physical changes within the 21-day cleansing period that follows each level of Reiki.

I approached a local Reiki master (Graham King) to discuss the Reiki way of healing and he offered to give me a treatment. I grilled Graham remorselessly about the system. He must have thought I was paranoid but, after an hour of interrogation, I trusted him enough to allow him to give me a treatment. I was used to receiving healing but the energy I felt that day was different to anything I had experienced before. It seemed to me that Reiki was felt more physically in the body than the soft gentle healing I was used to. I was intrigued enough to find out more and arranged to attend a workshop with Graham to have myself attuned to the Reiki energy. Eventually, I was so impressed with this new tool that I sat the Master/Teacher's level, which meant I could teach Reiki if I wished to do so.

Certificates and courses do not in themselves guarantee an effective healer, but they do at least show a willingness to work on ourselves, and a desire to be taken seriously. If the healer has taken courses with a recognised body, such as the National Federation of Spiritual Healers or the Reiki Federation, they will have to adhere to a code of conduct that helps to protect the patient. However, I believe that certificates should be backed up by good clinical experience.

One result of my attending a Reiki workshop and being attuned to the Reiki system of healing was that I appeared to be able to channel an increased amount of energy. Patients that I had worked with previously commented that they could feel more energy in their bodies. It also enabled me to see people's auras clearly; these new tools helped me to take the healing treatment to a different level. I could now see blocked energy in my patients' bodies and auras, and this enabled me to direct the healing energy into specific areas that needed help.

The other result of my qualification in Reiki has been that I can have two hats on when working at the hospital. Sometimes a patient, mainly for religious reasons, takes exception to the label 'spiritual healing', but I have found that they will often agree to receive Reiki. For me there is no difference; sometimes people will comment that Reiki is felt more physically in the body, but I do not change my treatment from Reiki to spiritual healing. It is the same treatment whatever the label. My earlier observations that Reiki seemed to be felt more physically is perhaps more a reflection that healing will give the patient whatever they need at that time. Sometimes that will be a soft, gentle, loving experience and sometimes it will be a more physical experience resulting in the physical relief of pain.

I believe there is only one God but many different routes to him – I also believe there is only one energy but many different ways of accessing it. It doesn't matter about patients' religious beliefs, they just need to be open to the 'healing process' for it to be of benefit to them. Having two hats means I can help more patients during my rounds.

CHAPTER 26

I remember very well when I first started to be aware of people's auras. I was giving a treatment to a patient in my healing room at home, when I suddenly became aware that I could see the energy field surrounding her physical body. I'd had a good cry the previous evening and thought at first that my eyes were the cause of the misty shape I could see. I rubbed my eyes and looked again, only to find I could see the smoky shape even more clearly.

As I looked at the patient I could see the energy flowing from my hand and making swirling patterns on her dark clothing. I was aware that the energy surrounding her body was a very thick, sticky grey around the head and also slightly lopsided. I continued channelling energy, concentrating on the head and heart area, and watched in amazement as the energy field surrounding her body balanced itself. As it did so I became aware of colour coming into her energy field: mostly blue, green and purple. It was an amazing first glimpse of the energy field and the colours of the aura, and since that first time I have become used to seeing the energy fields of my patients. It is a very useful tool to have when I meet a new patient, as the different colours of the aura give important information to the experienced healer, who will gain a deeper insight into a patient's energy field and how best to help the individual.

To understand energy fields and auras you must first think of yourself as an energy being. The physical body is the reality that most people are aware of, but we have at least seven other bodies radiating out from the physical. These bodies can be seen by some healers as a great orb of energy. In someone who is ill – emotionally, mentally or physically – the orb of energy will have dark areas within it or be off-centre. When a client comes for healing with a mental illness their energy field will often be hovering above them, so that they are literally out of their bodies with the resulting mental and physical detachment.

Within this pool of energy I can see the chakras. I can see seven chakras but many people say there are eight. Each chakra is a different colour – this is because colour vibrates at different frequencies and the major chakras vibrate at a different rate. I believe that being able to see the chakras gives me another very useful tool in my box, as it can suggest to me where the most important areas for healing are located. For children and animals it is not particularly useful as they are both such wonderfully simple beings to heal, and they soak up the energy like a sponge. However, for adults who have learned to hide their true feelings and have often been blocked in their energy systems for a very long time, some other tools are very useful.

There is so much to be said about the different levels of the chakras that this section will only give a brief outline of the functions and colour of each one. It is only if you wish to become a healer that a broader knowledge becomes necessary.

The *Crown Chakra* (located on the top of our head) vibrates to the colour magenta. At the physical level it is linked with the pineal gland; it can also affect the brain and has links to the rest of the body.

The *Brow Chakra* (located in the middle of our brow) vibrates to the colour violet. At the physical level it is linked to the hypothalamus and the pituitary gland. An imbalance here will affect the nerves of the head, the brain, the eyes and the face.

The *Throat Chakra* (located in the middle of the throat) vibrates to the colour blue. At the physical level it is linked to the thyroid and parathyroid glands, and can also affect the throat, neck, nose, mouth, teeth and ears.

The *Thymus Chakra* (located approximately 12cm (5 inches)

below the throat) vibrates to the colour turquoise. At the physical level it affects the immune system and therefore many of the problems that result from a lowered immune function. This is the chakra I cannot see.

The *Heart Chakra* (located between the breasts or pectorals) vibrates to the colour green. At a physical level it is linked to the thymus gland, also the heart, lungs, bronchial tubes, chest, upper back and arms.

The *Solar Plexus Chakra* (located above the navel) vibrates to the colour yellow. At the physical level it is linked to the pancreas, the digestive system, the liver, gall bladder, diaphragm and the middle back.

The *Sacral Chakra* (located beneath the navel) vibrates to the colour orange. At the physical level it is linked to our gonads (testes in the male, ovaries in the female). It also affects the urogenital organs, the womb, kidneys, lower digestive organs and the lower back.

The *Base Chakra* (located at the base of the spine) vibrates to the colour red. At the physical level it is linked to the endocrine system through the adrenal glands. Its energies affect the lower parts of the pelvis, along with the hips, legs and feet.

If you then begin to think of the different emotions that are also linked with these chakras (for example, the base chakra – our sense of belonging/survival/life-force) you will see how important it is for all our chakras to be balanced. This is a vital part of what a healer does, and by balancing your chakras the healer is assisting you in putting your body in the best possible position to heal. I don't explain all this to my patients, either in the hospital or in my healing room at home, but it can be useful for me to know more about what is out of balance with my patients, both physically and emotionally.

Many people have read self-help books these days and have worked through a lot of their problems, or so they think. When they turn up for an appointment bemoaning the fact that they are still stuck and not moving forward, it is very useful to use a pendulum to check which of their chakras are closed. This then gives me an insight emotionally as to why they may be blocked. They may have begun to understand their emotional wounds mentally and have felt they have cleared issues, but that is only in their mental body – the past hurt may still be resonating in their more subtle bodies. As this block is energetic, the only tool that will move it is energy.

The next stage I hope to reach is to be able to see spirit people. Again, this may sound slightly wacky, but I believe it can be done and I am very envious of people who can do it. I would dearly love to see Sam, but so far I have not. However, I often know he is present by the smell in the room. In the later stages of his life there was a particular scent that was around him, a sort of butterscotch smell, and I often smell it within the house and say 'hello', knowing that he is there.

When I gave a talk some time ago to a charity called Contact, who help the parents of children who have cancer, I was amazed by how many parents came up to me later to say that they had seen their children since they had died. Apparently they just appear in the house and disappear just as quickly. Now I have a greater understanding of energy I can relate to this more. I believe that the spirit world is all around us but vibrates at a faster rate than we do; this means our loved ones can be anywhere they like at any given time.

Knowing all of this should give me all the comfort I need, but in reality I miss Sam dreadfully and, like many other bereaved people, burst into tears when a particularly poignant tune comes on the radio. On the other hand, one of Sam's favourite songs was 'Brimful of Asha' by Cornershop, which includes the line 'Everybody needs a bosom to lean on'. When it is played on the radio now I have to laugh, as an image flashes through my mind of how he used to dance around to it being a little rude as was his way. I chat away to him believing that he can hear everything I say. I try very hard to be happy in my own life, as I know then that he is drawn to me only with love and therefore is free to come and go as he pleases.

It is this belief that I try to pass on to other grieving people. Yes, we miss them terribly, but death is only a separation and not an ending.

When I am working at the hospital with a carer who is facing the death of a loved one, especially if it's a parent facing losing a child, we will often spend time talking together. My experience with Sam usually helps them, even if it's just to let them know they are not alone and that I do understand what they are going through. I do not thrust the fact that I have lost a child down their throats, which would be inappropriate. But, if the subject has come up and we have talked about Sam, it usually helps them to know that their world will shake and rock on its axis but that – impossible as it seems at the time – life will go on for the rest of the family.

CHAPTER 27

The wards that I work on at UCLH make up the haematology unit with (currently) forty in-patient beds. Most patients are undergoing transplants of one sort or another, and we also have sickle-cell and thalassaemia patients, all of whom have problems with the blood.

When I was only working there for one day a week, my first job in the morning was to check the list of patients who were still in hospital from my last visit. If they had received healing the previous week they were first on my list for a treatment, as they invariably wanted to continue with the healing. Patients are usually in hospital for between six and ten weeks, though some unfortunately develop complications and have to stay longer. In the first few months of working on the wards I had tried to introduce as many patients as possible to healing. Now that the service was so popular that was no longer possible. The patients who had already used healing wanted to continue until their discharge, and this meant that a lot of patients missed out on the opportunity to try a session. There are only so many hours in a day and I focused on those patients who were already on my list and wanted ongoing treatments – I felt it would be better to really help as many of those as I could rather than spreading myself too thinly and not making as much of a difference to each patient as a result. Even though I now have more time at the hospital, my daily routine hasn't changed much.

Having established my list of patients for the day I visit them to see how they are and arrange a time to give a treatment. I work at the bedside, normally, in their own rooms, for several reasons: they are often attached to a pump that is delivering their medication; they may be feeling tired and unwell, and not keen to leave their rooms; and, as their treatment lowers their immune system to the point of neutropenia, it is safer for them to have a treatment in their own beds.

If a relative requires a treatment we do have a small side room to work from. This is very important, as the family member is less likely to release emotions when the patient is present. This privacy can be important for the patient, too – often this will be their first experience of healing and they may ask if the relative can stay, choosing to be alone only when they become more familiar with me and the treatment.

I know from my own experience that you want to appear to your loved one as strong and in control so that you can support them fully. However, I also know that it is vital to offer support to the relative, because if the supporter is helped then ultimately the patient is also helped.

I usually play music when I am giving a treatment. This is not strictly necessary for the session to be beneficial, but I find that, particularly in a medical setting, the music changes the atmosphere to one that is less institutional. I have a variety of music but the patient usually chooses something either relaxing or invigorating.

It was very amusing when I first started work on the ward as the consultants would often be on their rounds while I was healing. It seemed that they always used to come round just as we had started playing 'Sacred Spirit' (very powerful Native-American dance music). The look on the consultants' faces would amuse the patient hugely, but apart from a few mutterings under their breath the medics seemed happy enough. I am very fortunate that on our unit the medical staff are concerned only with how the patients benefit, and are very open to complementary therapy. I only hope that other hospitals can learn from this attitude.

Because the patients are so ill, the energy I channel is often felt in a very powerful way. As the energy hits an energy blockage the patient will literally shake and jerk as the energy tries to unblock the energy lines. I am very privileged to have witnessed the most profound happenings, and shared the most humbling and spiritual moments with the patients I treat. It is very rare for a patient in this setting to feel nothing at all – it is more usual for them to feel a lot of movement within the body and report seeing various colours and flashes of light When we discuss which colours they have seen, the colours will usually relate to the chakra that was blocked or the area within the body that a particular chakra controls.

One patient, who was a doctor undergoing a transplant for breast cancer, told me that she felt that the healing had put her back into balance and given her more clarity. She was one of those patients who commented that it was wonderful to be touched by someone who did not have a needle in their hand, and this validated for me my belief in as much hands-on healing as possible. Some healers only work off the body, but I believe we should never underestimate the power of touch.

The feedback that patients give me is astounding – several patients describe seeing loved ones who are already in spirit and, amazingly, some have told me that they have seen my son Sam. When I have questioned how they knew it was Sam they have described him very accurately, giving me a full description that left me in no doubt.

Ron Moulding (the medium I went to see) was able to shed some light on this when I asked him what it meant. He said that it did not mean, as I had feared, that these patients were going to pass into spirit, but simply that Sam was showing himself to me through them, to prove he was helping with the healing from the other side of life. I was taken aback by this news and once again overwhelmed by the power and love of Sam and the gift that he has given both to me and to these patients. I only saw Ron three times for a sitting, usually on Sam's birthday or at Christmas. Ron is very firm with clients that once they have received proof of 'life after life' they no longer need to see a medium but should be content to know that their loved one is safe and happy and get on with living their own lives.

I must admit I found this attitude hard to take in the beginning, but as time has gone by I can see the wisdom of it and admire Ron's stance, which validated his gift even more in my eyes.

I see on average ten patients a day and will often treat nursing staff at the end of my shift. I love working with the nurses; it is hugely rewarding to see their perception of healing change when they experience the energy for themselves. The nurses do an amazing job and are very committed to giving their patients the best possible care. If by receiving healing they have felt an improvement in their own bodies or lives, this will help them do their jobs even better. They are then also very proactive in encouraging their patients to try the healing on offer.

Because of the demanding nature of their job, the nurses often have stress-related illnesses: migraines, irritable bowel syndrome, etc. Staff can be very distressed when a patient they have nursed for a long time has died. They also feel the pain and grief, and it is wonderful to be able to help them spiritually.

At the end of my day's work at UCLH I would be shattered but elated. At home, though, since I filed for divorce things had become very tense between David and myself.

Charles was also becoming increasingly difficult to deal with as he felt that I was no longer interested in working with animals since beginning at the hospital. This was totally untrue, as I found working with animals very grounding – it is hard to get too full of yourself when you are up to your neck in mud in a field working on a pony with mud fever. We were still working together six days a week, but he began to be more and more controlling. The situation had become worse as I was now going to be a divorced woman; he apparently was frightened of me being, as he put it, 'footloose and fancy-free'.

Charles had many personal fears and insecurities and I constantly reassured him that I was committed to working in both fields, gently reminding him that we were business partners not life partners, but the situation continued to deteriorate. His moods were increasingly unpredictable and I wondered how long we could go on like this.

CHAPTER 28

Travelling around the country with Charles was often a roller-coaster ride for the emotions. We would have long spiritual conversations together in which Charles, having convinced me that Buster, his guide, was helping Sam settle in on the other side, would feed me details of Sam and his new life in the spiritual world. In hindsight I'm not sure how much of what he told me was true, but, typically, I was eager to hear as much of Sam as I could and convinced myself that it was true.

Now that Charles and I are no longer working together I can see that we were put together to help me through those terrible first years without Sam and I am grateful to Charles for all the teaching he gave me about working with the animals. When we arrived at our destination we would get on with the healing, working in complete harmony together. We held clinics in Nottinghamshire, Wales and Wiltshire, and there was always a queue of people and animals waiting to be seen.

The patients were a very interesting mix of small animals, horses, people and, on a few occasions, large bulls! Charles had been doing these clinics before he became ill and the animals and people had missed him. He introduced me to everyone as his new business partner and I was soon accepted as part of the team.

A normal day at our clinic in Wiltshire would be to arrive at 9 a.m. after an early start from Hertfordshire and find our list for the day included five humans, six horses and several small animals, ranging from a swan to a dog with a nasty tumour in his nose. The dog with the tumour was in quite a bad way – the tumour was obstructing his airway and every time he sneezed, blood would pour from his nose. We gave healing for a number of months and the tumour began to shrink. It never went away completely, but the dog regained its appetite and enjoyed more quality time with its owner before passing peacefully into spirit.

I was taught to recognise that if a lump was not fixed to the muscle or bone it was rarely cancer, but if it was fixed the chances were that it was. The treatment would always be the same: healing for four consecutive sessions to bring the disease under control, then monthly to keep the cancer dormant. We also advised owners to give their pets garlic, which Charles thought was very beneficial. Many of the animals we treated did have cancer and had been brought for healing as a last resort. The healing was very effective in prolonging and achieving quality of life as it had done for Sam. As I had with Sam, so I felt with all my patients, both human and animal – the more quality time spent with loved ones and relatives the better. If, by healing, we were providing that, then I thought it was worth it. Obviously Sam was never far from my thoughts when I was healing, either with Charles or at UCLH, and I would often smell the fragrance that I associated with him or feel the tug on my chin that I recognised as a sign that Sam was close (when Sam was still alive he would tease me that when I was having a strop I would stick my chin out, and he would often grab hold of it and give it a tug).

I particularly loved working with horses. I had been brought up in the countryside and had looked after other people's ponies when I was young. To give healing to a large animal such as a horse is a wonderful demonstration of energy. When you begin to channel energy into the animal's head, the horse will slowly lower its head to the ground and look as if it's about to nod off. Charles taught me to keep an eye open for this happening, as it's very embarrassing to have an expensive showjumper fall to the ground in front of its owner!

When people say to me, 'Ah yes, but healing is nothing more than a placebo effect', I always refer to the animals, to show that healing is obviously much more than that. As far as I know, the animals do not listen to what I'm saying about positive thoughts and do not meditate or visualise healing energy for their health, but nevertheless we get marvellous results. Charles advised me not to get too clever about healing and avoid getting embroiled with such details as where the animals' chakras are. I believe that healing for animals is really the purest form of unconditional love. He cautioned me to avoid people who became too cerebral in their thinking and, like me, preferred to be judged by the results we achieved for our patients, whether they be human or animal.

Healing on animals does have its fair share of dangers, as an animal does not necessarily appreciate the sensation of energy entering its body. An animal will often kick, bite or scratch in reaction to the healing, so an important part of the animal-healing courses that I teach is to recognise and understand the various signs that animals give us if they are becoming upset, to avoid any injuries to the healer. It is a very fulfilling field to work in and acts as a good balance to the intensely emotional work within the hospital.

The healing clinics were a wonderful learning ground for me as we saw a huge variety of animals and they gave me a broad spectrum of experience. Charles was very keen for me to carry on the business when he eventually passed into spirit but it didn't work out that way.

CHAPTER 29

I moved out of our family home in December 1999, sixteen months after Sam had died. Things had become increasingly tense between David and me, and it was obvious that the constant tension between us was beginning to affect Nick in a negative way. I remember only too well hearing my parents arguing and fighting when I was a child and I did not want to subject Nick to the same experience.

I decided to try and rent a house nearby that would suit me until I was in a position to buy again. I eventually found a house that I could afford which would, importantly, allow me to still work from home. The day I moved out it poured with rain, and I saw my new home as symbolic of how I was feeling at that time, standing alone in the middle of nowhere with no one around to support me.

Nevertheless there was a sense of relief at leaving the house where Sam had passed into spirit. We had moved there just as Sam had relapsed and I did not associate the house with happy family memories. The last thing I wanted to do was to make Nick choose between David and me and, for the time being, he chose to stay in the family home with David. However, my decision to stay close by was obviously based on being close to Nick whatever he chose. It was my choice to go it alone, and I felt I had to allow Nick to make up his own mind, without any pressure from me, as to where he wanted to live and with whom.

The house I rented really was all on its own in the middle of a field. Although it stood in a beautiful situation it was very unloved and run-down, having been rented for many years. The house was set high on a hill and the wind caught it from every angle. On my first night alone there the house groaned and moaned as the wind and rain beat against it from every direction, the doors and windows rattled like a hundred ghosts on the rampage and I lay in bed tossing and turning. I convinced myself that someone was trying to get in the back door and I lay there wondering what do. Eventually I realised that I could either go downstairs and challenge any intruder that might be there, or I could roll over and go to sleep. I decided to go to sleep, reasoning that if anyone was in the house they would soon see there was nothing of value and hopefully go away. I awoke the next morning perfectly rested, and resolved never to feel nervous from that point on.

Charles Siddle and I had by now parted and gone our separate ways. Things had come to a head when he began telling me who was a suitable friend for me and who was not! He told me that Buster, his guide, was advising him what was best for me, and when I did not accept this we had a blazing row. I suppose I was getting stronger again and could see people more clearly, Charles reminded me of my own father, who had always been very domineering, and although I believed Charles was only acting so outrageously because of his insecurities, the situation could not be allowed to go on. We had a parting of the ways and our business together was brought to a close.

In hindsight I can see that all these experiences were making me stronger, but at the time it all felt too much. In addition to everything else going on in my life at the time, I was now potentially in trouble financially, as I would be completely self-supporting from this point on. Having just moved to a new house with rent to pay, I had now lost the work that would have paid for it.

I made an appointment to speak to Stephen Rowley, who was now my immediate line manager at the hospital (Tim Jackson had moved to another hospital). I explained that my circumstances had changed and that I might have to look for other work to supplement what I was doing. Stephen immediately offered me another full day's work at the hospital – he was incredibly supportive of my work and had been ready to offer me another day as soon as his budget allowed. From the patients' point of view it was a very positive development, as the ones I was already treating would be able to have two treatments a week and I would hopefully be able to treat some new patients too. I knew from my healing with Sam that the more healing a seriously ill person receives the better the effect will be.

Christmas came and went that first year on my own, without a great deal of joy. Nick came up to the cottage for Christmas lunch but it was a difficult day for him – not only were we without Sam for the second year, but now his parents were living in separate houses. He never complained, but it must have been very difficult for him. Now, when we speak about those times, he doesn't remember feeling upset about his life and the way it was going; he seems to have an amazing ability to accept whatever is happening. Sometimes we as adults project our own thoughts and feelings onto our children but, as Nick has proved, they are often dealing with things in their own way and are stronger than we think emotionally.

During those last few months that I was at home Nick asked me for healing, and at last I was able to help him by releasing some of the emotional trauma from the past three years. The healing also gave us space to be together and without doubt brought us even closer. I had also offered healing to David but he had never wanted to use it for himself – maybe there was a part of him that wasn't ready to release the pain, choosing to box it up and not look at it.

I was feeling particularly low over the Christmas holidays and felt drawn to take a trip up to Walsingham in Norfolk to the famous shrine where we had taken Sam for healing. The shrine was empty, of course, as everybody was together in their homes enjoying Christmas with their families. I sat miserably in the chapel and tried to tune into Sam, asking how he was and whether he was having a happy Christmas. I shed some tears of self-pity and then got up and wandered around the shrine. As I was leaving my eye was caught by a statue of Our Lady with a dagger inserted in her heart. It was exactly how I felt and I left the chapel feeling very sorry for myself.

There were only a few shops in Walsingham open that day and I noticed that one had a picture of a small child in the window. It was obvious to me that the child had undergone chemotherapy and I went inside to look around at the goods on sale. I spoke to the woman behind the counter and asked about the child in the picture. I was taken aback when she said it was her child and the little girl had died the previous year. I felt a rush of emotion and before I knew it we were sharing experiences of our beautiful brave children.

There were so many similarities: her daughter was also ten when she died and had been diagnosed with the same type of leukaemia as Sam, and the woman had taken her child to see many of the healers that Sam and I had visited. It was quite extraordinary the amount of similarities between us. Her daughter also owned a Jack Russell puppy and they had been devoted to each other just like Sam and Zack.

This meeting reminded me that I was not alone and that there are many, many people who are sad and distressed about losing a loved one and having to carry on with their lives. We continued to talk and the tears began to fall; we hugged each other for comfort. I suddenly realised that, while it's all right to feel sorry for yourself occasionally, life for the rest of the family has to go on. That's where I should have been, at home in my new house with Nick, who must have been missing Sam every bit as much as me, not here in Walsingham feeling sorry for myself. I drove back to Hertfordshire with new purpose in my step. I might be on my own, but I still had Nick and I had work to do.

CHAPTER 30

It seemed that something important had shifted within me after that Christmas visit to Walsingham. Ever since Sam's death I had very much wanted to work with children alongside my work with adults but, since it is mainly adults on the wards at UCLH, I very rarely did. Now it seemed there were suddenly a lot of children on my list of patients to see at home.

One of the first was a young girl called Karly. Her parents, Julie and Paul, had read an article about the work I did at University College Hospital and rang me to see if I could help their daughter. That first contact was made because the medical team at Great Ormond Street Hospital had told the family that there was no longer anything they could do for their daughter. Naturally they were devastated.

I told them that, while I could offer no miracles, I was very happy for them to bring Karly to my healing room in Hertfordshire. Karly was ten and had been ill for a year – she had suffered a stroke as a complication of her treatment and had been left with no speech and very little movement. The day Karly arrived at my home was a very special one for me. As her parents brought her into my room and laid her onto the healing couch, I felt a surge of energy within my body as if to confirm that I would be able to help her in some way. I explained to her family what the healing session would involve and they sat quietly in the room while I worked on their daughter. When I begin to channel energy I will often sense where the patient's pain is without being told, but in this case I was quickly able to reassure Karly's parents that she was in no physical pain.

This was a great relief to them as they feared she might be suffering and be unable to tell them because of the stroke. When I had finished the treatment Karly looked very peaceful and Julie commented that Karly had made eye contact with her (which she very rarely did) when she had lifted her off the couch.

I offered healing to Julie and Paul, not only because I know that parents and carers also need help, but also because I like parents to sample the healing so that they can be reassured that their children are receiving something tangible. This is easily validated by the energy they can feel in their own body during a treatment. A healing session can bring a profound sense of calm and will help focus the mind when someone is deeply stressed. Over the following months Paul, who had initially been very sceptical, decided to experience healing, encouraged by his wife and elder daughter Anna who had already undergone it. Much to his surprise he felt the energy strongly in his legs and knees. I was able to explain to him that the energy was working on the emotional level as well as the physical. Legs and knees are about strength, flexibility and the ability to move forward with our emotional difficulties. Paul had also sustained damage to his knee in the past that I was not aware of but the energy also showed me that the healing was needed physically in that area, so for him it was confirmation that Karly was indeed benefiting from the healing and that if she had been in pain I would have known it.

Over the subsequent months we all got to know each other very well, and when Karly passed into spirit her parents decided that they would like to see the medium whom I had visited after Sam's death. On that first reading Karly came through straightaway with confirmation that she was well and happy on the other side of life. She also confirmed what I had told her parents, that she had been in no pain before her death. During the reading they received from Ron they were told that Karly had met up with a young boy called Sam in spirit; this was more proof for me that Sam and I were still working well as a team, me on this side and Sam on the other.

I never speak to Ron about the patients I see, as I know how important it was to me that the medium knew nothing about my family before I went for that first reading with Sam. I would not attempt to manipulate people's lives by giving Ron any information. I realise that many people reading this will think it is all very far-fetched, but it is a validation of Ron's very strong gift that he has helped many hundreds of people over the years, giving wonderful evidence of life continuing beyond life on earth.

One of the many children that I began to see at my healing room was a young boy of nine who was suffering from acute migraines. Eddie was brought to me in desperation by his mother Meg, who told me that he was having a migraine attack every three days or so with heavy vomiting. Eddie was taking huge doses of painkillers and his life was very difficult. Doctors had run a battery of neurological tests and Eddie had been advised to have his eyes tested (which he had done) and had also been advised to change his diet. The tests revealed that there was nothing physical for the doctors to treat and yet Eddie was still in great pain. After the first session of healing (a routine session as previously described) Eddie's mum rang me to report that the headaches had stopped. I advised her to bring Eddie back the following week to consolidate the first treatment.

Healing for children is very similar to treating animals, as both are very open to healing and in general are very easy to work with, often responding in what seems like a miraculous fashion. A child has not had a lifetime of learning to cover up their emotions, therefore the energy blockages can be released very quickly. Eddie came for a further two treatments to make sure the migraines were a thing of the past and then went onto a maintenance programme where he only came for a treatment if things were becoming stressful at school. It is, of course, immensely fulfilling to be able to help children in this way and a part of my work that I love. I do not charge for healing children, preferring to see it as a gift to them from Sam.

I have seen many children in my healing room at home, but I look forward to the day when healing can be offered to children in hospital alongside conventional medicine as we do for the adults at UCLH. While there are no really young children being treated on the unit where I work, there are often teenagers on the ward as we have four beds dedicated to the Teenage Cancer Trust. I am always very aware that it is probably more difficult to be ill when you are a teenager, as it is such a traumatic age. Not only are you still trying to discover who you are, but self-image is vital to you and to lose your hair must be a bitter blow.

One young girl that I remember fondly was Sarah. She would have nothing to do with me or the healing for some time, then one day when she was particularly fed up she asked to see me. The nurses had warned me that she was angry and hostile, refusing to eat or to come out of her room. I steeled myself, knocked on the door and went into her room. I felt like Daniel going into the lions' den!

Sarah was sitting up in bed watching me carefully (checking me out for signs of fear!). I smiled cheerfully and asked whether she wanted to talk or just receive the treatment. Sarah chose the treatment, and so without a word I set up my music and began the healing. Sarah didn't move or say a word throughout the thirty-minute session but afterwards, as I began to gather up my bits and pieces to leave, she opened her eyes and asked when I was coming again. I said I would return if she wanted when I was next in and she grunted a reply and rolled over. I was dismissed!

Later on that day a nurse came rushing up to me saying, 'It's a miracle!' I was used to some of the staff having a joke with me, but asked what the miracle was. The nurse said that shortly after my session with Sarah she had rung her bell demanding some food and had come out into the dayroom to mix with some of the other teenagers on the ward. In a way it was a miracle. To have Sarah come out of her room and not to be lying miserably in her bed was something to be proud of.

Often with healing we have to be content with a small but important change for the better, but one that, at that moment, makes a big difference to the person's life. Sarah continued to receive healing twice a week for her the rest of her stay in hospital and was very keen to continue with healing after her discharge.

I wish more patients would access a healer after discharge from hospital. In my opinion it is very useful to use healing as a recovery tool, as can be demonstrated by Katie.

Katie was someone I already knew when she came for her first healing session. She had been in Great Ormond Street Hospital at the same time that Sam was being treated there. Katie had been diagnosed with leukaemia when she was ten, but with a type that had a better prognosis than Sam's disease. Nevertheless Katie had relapsed and had just undergone a transplant when we met up again; she was thirteen. Her leukaemia was in remission but unfortunately she was in a very weak and depleted state as a result of her treatment.

Her mother Lesley Anne thought healing was, in her words, 'A load of old twaddle', but feels very differently now. Lesley Anne brought Katie to me because, despite being in remission after a successful transplant, she was having great trouble eating normally. She could not eat enough to sustain her and she would often vomit the food that she had managed to swallow. She was very lethargic and unfortunately had to be fed via a nasal gastric tube (a tube inserted up her nose and down her throat to her stomach).

I gave Katie a routine treatment that Friday and sent the family on their way. The following Monday I received a call from Lesley Anne who asked me what had I done to her child. I cautiously asked her what the problem was. She replied that Katie had been eating her out of house and home ever since that first visit, having asked for fish and chips on the way home from my house the previous Friday!

Lesley Anne has now become a great advocate for healing, often sending others to me if she feels healing will be of benefit to them. She believes, as I do, that healing should be available at every cancer hospital and clinic throughout the country. Katie says her visits to me are 'very relaxing and I always comes away feeling happy'.

Katie continued to come for regular sessions and she became stronger and stronger until eventually she was no longer a girl who had been very ill but a beautiful young woman who was well again. I was out shopping one Saturday when a familiar face caught my eye in Boots. Katie was behind the checkout doing a normal Saturday job while she sat her A levels at school. I was delighted to see her and very touched to have been a part of her recovery. Lesley Anne often asked me if I found it difficult seeing other children get better when Sam had not. I can honestly say that I do not. I am just so delighted when anybody gets well and stays well – it makes what I do as a healer worthwhile.

CHAPTER 31

My personal life was a lot calmer now that I was living alone, and I believe the energy I was able to channel became stronger because of this. I firmly believe that to be an effective healer you have to be honest with yourself. If there are emotional or physical issues that you are aware of, it is only truthful to work to try and clear them; anything less would be hypocritical of me.

Working with my own pain was difficult, as my heart had unsurprisingly closed down over the past few years and now I had to work hard to clear the emotional blockage and open my heart once again. I advise my clients that if we are to attract the right partner, we have to work on ourselves to help bring this about. Like attracts like, and if I wanted a partner in my life with an open heart, then I had to work on my own.

During the year since I had left home my interest in the Reiki energy grew. I began to use my own style of healing, taking what I considered the best of my training as a spiritual healer and mixing it with the best of Reiki. I began to attend regular meditation classes to help heal myself, and found meditation to be a very powerful self-healing tool.

One of the classes I attended was run by the Reiki Master who had attuned me to Reiki the previous year, Graham King. Graham became a good friend over the year and reflected a lot of my positive qualities back at me, but he also mirrored a lot of my remaining blocks. It was an interesting time recognising that the very things that irritated me most about him were qualities that I still had to work on with myself. I find this a useful thing to bear in mind if someone comes into my life who I find difficult to deal with. I usually ask myself the question, 'Where in my life am I still acting like this?' Sometimes, though, it is worth remembering that it can be just the other person's baggage, and nothing to do with you!

Over the following year Graham and I grew closer, finally admitting our growing feelings for each other. It was very difficult at first. It has been said that the price of great love is great grief and I had already experienced that. I was opening my heart to feel love again and I was initially very frightened.

Now Graham and I are settled in our new life, I can appreciate how good it is to be with someone who understands the work that I do, and who shares the same interests. David has also found a new partner and seems more content. Nick accepted Graham, saying that he was relieved at my choice, and at least I hadn't picked a biker clad in leather! In an ideal world it would have been good to have stayed in a marriage for life, but in an ideal world Sam would never have become ill and died. Some things are just not meant to be.

I find that my own personal difficulties have helped me in my healing work. To me there is nothing worse than a cheerful person telling you that they know how you feel, when it is quite obvious they haven't a clue how you feel and have never experienced what you are going through. I don't maintain that I know how everyone I treat feels, but at least I can begin to empathise with them better, given my own history.

Many of my private clients arrive at my door having read a lot of self-help books; often they are very aware of their problems but are unable to move on from them. The books that they have read have helped them, but often only to understand their problems mentally. The negative experiences they are trying to shift can be found still resonating in the outer levels of their aura, and therefore often manifesting themselves in the physical body. For all their hard work they are still as 'stuck' as they have ever been. As part of their healing session I will check their energy centres and aura to find the source of the blocked energy. As I have said before, blocked energy needs an energy tool to release it; this is where healing comes in.

One such client, Anne, came to me with a chronic neck problem. She had been to an osteopath with no success and eventually, in desperation, had found her way to my door. When I suggested to her that her neck problem may have an emotional cause she readily agreed, bursting into tears and talking at length about the emotional difficulties within her family. Having unburdened herself verbally the energy session was able to begin. A routine check of her chakras revealed (unsurprisingly) several energy blocks, and as the session continued her body began to release the blocked energy with very strong physical twitching. This is very common and, as I have mentioned previously, is a sign that the energy being channelled is trying to reopen the energy lines. After four sessions Anne's neck problem had completely resolved itself; furthermore, she now had the insight to avoid any potential emotional flash points that would start the problem off again.

If we know ourselves well, we can manage our own lives better and learn to avoid negative thoughts and life patterns, which may result in a problem manifesting itself physically. I am a firm believer that the client and healer work together and if, on rare occasions, clients are unwilling to help themselves, their physical problem may reappear after a year or so. I believe that for healing to take place at the source of the problem you have to work at these deeper levels; otherwise you are in danger of simply 'putting a sticking plaster on the wound'. One of the great rewards of working with people at these deeper levels is when you see a person's life completely change for the better.

Coral was a young mother who initially brought her child to me for healing. During the healing session on her child, Coral became upset and I gently suggested she might like to get some help for herself, via friends or her GP. Coral was not keen on either of these routes and decided instead she would like to come for a healing session. During the many sessions that Coral had over the following months a very difficult childhood emerged, and the difficulties she had experienced had followed her into adult life, resulting in deep unhappiness and quite severe panic attacks. It was wonderful to see the new stronger Coral emerge as she unburdened the emotional baggage from the past. Coral became very interested in Reiki and went on to become a Reiki healer herself. On one occasion, when she was sitting outside a supermarket unable to bring herself to go in due to a panic attack, she was able to give herself a short Reiki treatment. It was, for her, nothing short of miraculous that she was then able to complete her shopping and go home without any further problems. No doubt Coral's own very difficult life experiences have made her a very empathic healer for many people as well as a stronger person in supporting her child.

CHAPTER 32

Working at the hospital has been the most amazing experience, and I am privileged to see the most wonderful demonstrations of energy on the patients I treat there. As I've said before, I feel this is probably because the patients at the hospital are so ill that the effect of healing is very dramatic. One client group that this is especially noticeable on is the 'sickle cell' patients. In simple terms sickle-cell disease means that some of the blood cells distort into a sickle shape, which results in the distorted cells accumulating in different parts of the body, creating a blockage. The resulting pain is impossible for most of us to imagine.

When a patient is admitted into hospital with a 'sickle-cell crisis' they are immediately administered intravenous painkillers. Over the years the pain relief can becomes less effective, resulting in having to use ever stronger opiates to control the pain. It is a terrible condition to live with, and for most of the patients they have been doing this for most of their lives. It was difficult at first for me to get these patients to try healing because they were used to managing their painful sickle-cell crises with conventional treatments. However, over the months I began to build a relationship with one of the patients, Jilma.

We chatted about our children and other unrelated subjects, and eventually Jilma decided she had nothing to lose by trying healing. That first session was a revelation to us both – as soon as I touched her she went into an altered state and only returned when I gently shook her awake. When we talked about what she had experienced she said that she had felt no pain for the whole of the session and was pain-free for some time afterwards. This was a major breakthrough, as nothing at that time was able to help Jilma's pain; the healing gave her some small respite and she continues to use healing whenever she is an inpatient.

With the kind of pain these patients suffer I feel very strongly that they should be able to access healing as an ongoing supportive therapy. At present they are only able to have it on an ad hoc basis, i.e. when they are in-patients having a crisis. It would be wonderful to be able to offer healing to them when they are in their out-patient clinics – in this way perhaps we could see some improvement in their daily lives as well as when they are in crisis. I have been privileged to work with many sickle-cell patients and we now have a mutual respect for each other.

Jamie is a man in his prime with a young fiancée, and he should have had his whole world in front of him. However, he has lived with sickle cell for a very long time and then developed cancer, which resulted in him having to have a leg amputated as a complication of his disease. On the surface Jamie seems to be handling this very difficult situation admirably, but when he is receiving healing his body tells a very different story. Jamie has always loved the healing sessions, loving the release he gets from the altered state he enters. His physical body changes completely, and all of his repressed emotions begin to release in a very physical way. I have already mentioned the different levels that a healer works at, and this is never more apparent than when working on Jamie.

On one occasion, shortly after the amputation, he received healing while his fiancée was in the room. I had explained to her that Jamie's body may twitch and jerk as the healing unblocked all the trapped emotions, but we were both surprised at the amount of movement that occurred. Jamie's whole body convulsed with the trauma that was trapped in his energetic body and the stump of his amputated leg waved around in midair as the energy flowed through it.

I felt very moved, as it was so apparent how much Jamie had

courageously been hiding from his loved ones and yet how damaged he really was on an emotional level. After the session was completed I roused Jamie and asked how he felt. He replied that he felt fine and was aware of being very calm and hardly moving throughout the treatment. I looked at his fiancée and we both burst out laughing! Nothing could have been further from the reality of his body jerking about all over the place.

I have witnessed this amazing response many times, when people say they felt no movement when the opposite has been true. Though there is no scientific proof of why this is, I can only assume that if the patient had been conscious of the pain being released it would have been too much to bear, hence the altered state that some patients enter into.

Jamie loves the healing and describes it as the biggest rush he has ever experienced, saying he feels re-energised after a treatment. His fiancée is now so interested that she has decided to look further into healing herself. This would be wonderful, as she would be able to help Jamie on a daily basis with his pain and I'm sure this would bring them even closer than they already are.

One of the hardest things that I deal with at the hospital is when I see a family suffering and, for whatever reason, the patient is not open to healing. It is hard for me to stand and do nothing but wait until the situation changes and the family asks for healing. Healing works best on patients who are open to it, so it is best (as I had found with Nick) to wait until they decide to go ahead with it themselves.

One such patient was Christopher; he was extremely unwell with an illness that he had been living with for many years. I had passed his frantic wife many times in the corridor and had to bite my tongue not to interfere in their lives until I was asked. The door was opened into Christopher's room via an unexpected route. I had been asked a couple of times to appear on the *Kilroy* show and I had always refused, not because I am afraid to speak up for what I do, but because I did not want healing to be ridiculed in the way that it often is on these types of show. My work is much too important to me to have it made into entertainment for somebody. Anyway, when

I was approached a third time I agreed to appear (a little rule I have for myself is that if a situation comes up three times you are not meant to ignore it). I appeared on the show and Christopher saw me. He felt that if I was on TV I must be good and so he began to have healing!

Healing for Christopher turned out to be more than he had ever expected and he became a devoted fan, using it regularly alongside his conventional treatments. On one occasion he was admitted with an obstructed bowel and was unable to have an operation because of his frail physical condition. Doctors thought that he would die within a few days, but miraculously the bowel recovered and he was able to go home again. I am glad that I had the opportunity to help.

The rejection of healing is something I face on a daily basis at the hospital and I always find it hard not to offer help until it is asked for. However, the more patients come across healing being offered, the more they will feel it is 'normal' to ask to try it, and hopefully the more people will have access to the amazing power and results that healing can bring.

CHAPTER 33

I have worked with many, many patients over the years at the hospital and have become very close to some. I will never forget any of them, whether they are well or whether they have passed into spirit. But occasionally there is a patient that you connect with completely and they begin to feel like one of the family. One such patient for me was Matt.

I first met Matt at the hospital. He had been admitted after a routine blood test had shown some 'suspicious cells'. This is not unusual with the kind of leukaemia Matt had; unbeknown to me at that time, he had the same type of leukaemia as Sam, and a relapse was always a possibility. Matt had undergone a bone-marrow transplant and, despite a difficult time, he had been well for some years. It was therefore a terrible blow to the whole family for Matt to have relapsed.

Matt was 32 when I met him and was working as a fireman. His wife worked as a policewoman and they had two young children. When I walked into his room that first day I knew only that he had relapsed and might be in need of a bit of help.

Matt later told me that he only agreed to receive healing that day because he was so bored and frustrated with waiting to know what was going to happen next; he thought a session might at least pass the time! I explained what a treatment would involve and he shrugged his shoulders and said that I should go ahead. This was not a very auspicious start to what was going to be an amazing journey for both of us. I often choose music intuitively when I am working and that day I chose Native-American music for Matt. He smiled happily at my choice.

There was nothing unusual in that first healing session. It was very powerful, but then that is usual for patients when they are very ill. Matt, however, had never felt anything like it before and questioned me closely about the feelings that he was experiencing. We talked for a long time that day about how the doctors had to speak in terms of statistics, and how devastating this can be for the patient who is being told that there is nothing more to be done.

I spoke of my own belief that each one of us is an individual, and that we will respond to treatments in a way that can often be a surprise to the medics. As Matt had young children of his own he asked me about my children and I explained that I have two sons, one in spirit and one here with me. We discussed my belief that we continue to live on after our physical body has gone, and much to my surprise he said that he knew this, as when he had been ill previously he had an out-of-body experience.

We had many spiritual talks during this time, and we both learned a lot from each other, but it was not until the sixth session that something remarkable started to happen.

The session began like every other until I reached Matt's feet, and then quite out of the blue I felt a huge surge of energy pulse through my body. At the same time Matt's feet began to lift off the bed without any help from me whatsoever. I watched in amazement as his feet continued to hover above the bed as the energy poured through me and into Matt. I thought briefly to myself that this was going to look very peculiar to any nurse that may walk in the door at that moment, but was so excited at what was happening that I carried on with the session until I felt it was complete.

When I had finished the session I roused Matt. He looked at me in disbelief and asked if his feet had come off the bed. I said they had and we both laughed. He said, 'That's not all that happened,' and began to tell me all the things he had experienced. Apparently, when Matt had had his near-death experience, he had seen a circle of people above him and had been aware of floating above his body. In this latest healing he had experienced exactly the same thing but had also been aware of a Native-American chief in the circle of people he had seen. At this point we were interrupted by the doctors on their rounds, so I made my excuses and said I would pop back later.

When I returned later that day, Matt's wife Wendy had arrived for her visit. She said later that we were both like excited children, having shared an experience that to her seemed strange to say the least! Matt was discharged from hospital soon after that experience. The doctors could do nothing more for him but he was, at the time, well and was able to get on with his life.

Matt was now an out-patient, and began to come to my house in Hertfordshire for healing. We were both intrigued to see if the levitation of his feet had been a one-off, or whether it would happen again. If anything the healing was even stronger, perhaps because Matt could relax more knowing that no one was going to interrupt us, and the sessions became more and more powerful.

After one particular session, when levitation had occurred throughout his whole body, he commented to me that we must try and get this on film as it was so amazing. He had apparently been down the pub with his work colleagues and told them of his experience. Of course, they didn't believe him and he wanted to be able to show them himself. We arranged to video a session and, much to our amazement, we did capture his body levitating on the tape. We were both very excited by this and showed the tape to our families and friends, and I began to try and find out more about levitation.

I could find no real information via the usual channels so I consulted with my friend and medium, Ron Moulding. I asked him why we were experiencing this amazing healing when it was clear to me that, although Matt's spiritual body was growing ever stronger, his physical body was becoming weaker because the leukaemia was still active. Ron replied that the levitation was not about curing Matt but just to show him what was possible, and that nothing was impossible. Matt could then use this as knowledge to help himself, but more importantly it showed Matt that there was life after death, as demonstrated by the circle of people within the light that Matt often saw while receiving healing. Ron felt sure that this knowledge would take away any fear of death, if that was what was to come.

During this time Matt travelled to America with his family. Matt's wife Wendy says that it was thanks to the healing that Matt had enough energy to go on this trip, which they both felt would not have been possible otherwise. They were able to have many experiences that would be laid down as wonderful memories for the years to come. Matt was a complete convert to healing – he had begun treatment as a sceptic and now was one of healing's greatest advocates.

As Matt was now a private patient, we were able to work at an even deeper level than I was able to at the hospital, and because of this he began to address issues from his past that were still bothering him. Matt began to talk to his closest family about how he felt, that life was all about showing love to each other and being able to receive love. I know that over the following months Matt became the healer for his whole family. Even when he had to spend some time briefly in a hospice, Matt would greet all his visitors with wide outstretched arms and talk to them about love and the importance of showing it to everyone you cared for.

I personally was so proud of him; he made an enormous transition spiritually during those last months and even formalised his beliefs by taking the first steps to becoming a healer by learning Reiki (this was our gift to him as a special friend). He was then able to give himself treatments that he found beneficial in between seeing me for regular treatments. When he came out of the hospice for his last weeks at home, Graham and I were invited over for dinner to thank us for all we had done for him.

I will never forget that evening. Wendy had gone to a great deal of trouble to give us a splendid meal and Matt sat there tucking in with the best of us, and it must have taken enormous strength for him to have done that. It was Graham who fell asleep on the sofa that night, while Matt was still going strong despite his frail physical condition.

This for me is the essence of healing – not, unfortunately, always to be able to heal the physical body, but to offer strength and positivity, and therefore to be able to live every day to the fullest as Matt was doing, and as Sam had done.

A week later I was getting ready to go to work and was startled by a little bird flying right up to the window as I washed. Birds can often act as messengers from spirit, and I believe this bird had come to tell me to prepare myself. I knew at once that Matt would pass into spirit that day. Matt had asked if I would be with him when he passed, and I had agreed to be there.

I went off to work in London and, sure enough, later in the afternoon I received a call from Wendy, saying Matt had asked for me and would I come. I drove up to Hertford with mixed feelings: happy that Matt was going to be free as he had wanted to be for some time now, but also very sad that I was going to lose the physical presence of someone I cared about.

I believe that there is a role for healing right up to and beyond the time of dying. I have received so many messages from my patients (via mediums) who have passed away, saying that they had felt no fear at the time of passing and were able to walk away from their physical body and meet their loved ones with no remaining illness in their body. Though some people find what mediums do difficult to believe, I do believe it and it has given me a lot of strength to know that I am helping these people.

When I arrived at Matt and Wendy's home, Matt greeted me with a smile. Although heavily sedated, he knew that I was there. When Matt passed away some hours later it was perhaps as most of us would wish for; all his loved ones were there, including his children, and he quietly slipped away.

Matt's brother in Australia rang later that night and said that he had seen Matt in his garden at the exact moment of passing, proof again that life goes on and our loved ones can be where they want to be at any given time – they are free.

CHAPTER 34

The healing service continued to go from strength to strength and I was given a third day's work on the ward – this was a huge breakthrough as I could organise my week more effectively and introduce more patients to the benefits of healing alongside their conventional treatments.

There are many people with whom I have worked who have taken a little bit of my heart with them when they have passed into spirit, but there are many more I have worked with who are alive and well despite having had very difficult times. One of my patients that I am still in contact with is Linda.

I was asked to see Linda by one of the nurses on the ward. When I entered her room she looked up at me and asked if I was the pain lady. This was not a name I was used to, but was apparently the description the nurse had given her as to what I did with healing. I explained that while I hoped that the healing would indeed take away some of her pain, I could only do my best and we would have to wait and see. Linda was in too much pain for much of a discussion to take place, so I set up my music and began the treatment.

Linda had been diagnosed with non-Hodgkin's lymphoma and had already received chemotherapy and radiotherapy. She was in a great deal of pain that first day I met her and after explaining to her that I was not the pain-control specialist, but a healer, she said she didn't care what I was as long as I helped her with the pain.

I wasted very little time on explanations, simply saying that I would be touching her body very gently and would talk to her again when I had finished the treatment. I was aware of a great deal of energy that day and afterwards Linda opened her eyes in astonishment and began to tell me what she had experienced. She said she had seen (behind her closed eyes) a lot of pink and red images and experienced a strong sensation of pins and needles, along with a sense of lightness throughout her body.

Linda's pain had gone after the treatment and she continued to use healing twice a week during her stay in hospital. She had been told that she could expect to lose a lot of weight during her treatment, but she was very proud of the fact that she didn't lose a pound! Linda believes that the healing played a big part in her disease going into remission and says that the doctors are wonderful – but she also believes that you need all the help you can get to defeat a disease like cancer, and I would be the first to agree with her.

As I said, the further day's work at the hospital means that I have so much more time in which patients, relatives and staff can receive healing if they wish. In addition to my healing role, I have taken on the role of manager of the complementary therapy team. By taking this next step I hope to be able to expand the team's services into other areas within the trust, particularly within oncology, as we will be in the same building when our new hospital opens in 2005.

I hope there will be many more units such as ours in the future; we are justly proud of the care we offer our patients in what is now the biggest transplant unit in Europe. As a team we currently offer reflexology and massage five days a week, healing three days a week and hypnotherapy three days a week, as well as the usual counselling services three days a week. We are the face of modern medicine, integrating the very best of science with the holistic care that complementary therapies can offer.

Our team is fortunate to be paid for our services and although some of our funding comes from the NHS some also comes from the direct fundraising for the unit through the efforts of its dedicated fundraiser Sara Goldman. We are constantly looking for sponsors in order to expand our services. Many large companies are happy to donate money for specialist machines, which are invaluable, but I would also like them to consider sponsoring therapy time for the patients – both in our hospital and elsewhere – that would enable us to further expand our service.

CHAPTER 35

If you are following your own personal journey, whether it is through your own or someone else's illness, pain or discomfort, my advice would be to have an open mind and look at various therapies that appeal to you. If something is too much like hard work to arrange then you are probably going to become stressed, which would defeat the object. There is, after all, a life to be lived no matter what your prognosis is – enjoy it!

The following pages are not just intended for people who are dealing with a diagnosis of cancer. They will be equally helpful whatever your problem. Some of the conditions I have helped successfully over the years include cancer, sickle-cell, chronic fatigue syndrome (ME), multiple sclerosis, Crohn's disease, irritable bowel syndrome, depression, psychological and emotional issues, infertility, arthritis, migraine, eczema, asthma, back, knee and joint problems and many more. While I believe many of our problems can be traced to an emotional cause, this is, of course, not true for everybody. There are occasions when our physical body breaks down because of environmental or diet-related issues, or sometimes we simply have an accident. I would just like you to remember that you are more than a physical body and often healing of the physical requires us to work on the emotions.

I find the work I do with adults fascinating, as normally there are so many barriers to get through before we uncover the source of the problem. This is not always the case – some adults are very uncomplicated – but that is the exception rather than the rule. With adults you do have some advantages, though. You can ask them to do 'homework' and carry on the healing in between sessions, if they are willing to do this, and they will be amazed at the results they can achieve for themselves.

Unlike children, who have not yet formed many negative patterns, adults have usually been following negative patterns for a long time. I believe unless we deal with these unhealthy emotional and physical patterns the 'healing' will be little more than a 'sticking plaster' on the problem.

I have seen many people over the years and the ones who get well and stay well are the people who change things within their lives. I fully appreciate that some patterns are very difficult to break, but the reward is well worth the effort. After all, 'If we always do what we have always done, we will always get what we have always got.' A marketing expression, maybe, but very appropriate.

This is not a matter of making the patient feel guilty or responsible for their problems, it is about knowing ourselves and recognising what is healthy or unhealthy for us (for example, an addiction or an unhealthy relationship).

When I ask people to begin to think of themselves first, I am often told that this is a very selfish thing to do. I have to explain to them that if they are feeling good about themselves then the people around them will feel the benefit, and I remind them of the expression, 'God helps those who help themselves'. So many of our illnesses come from suppressed emotions. Having learned this, I looked back into my own history and my own family – women in our family were used to 'putting up and shutting up'. However, we also have a history of cancer within our family that would make your blood chill. Anybody who knows me will tell you that I definitely don't put up and shut up and I believe that by breaking the female pattern of behaviour within my family I will have helped to avert any threat to my health. This philosophy is only a part of fighting any illness, but a very important part nevertheless.

One of the most useful ways of shifting our patterns of behaviour is to work with affirmations. An affirmation is a positive statement said over and over to yourself (even more effective if done while looking into a mirror) and they are a wonderful tool into the subconscious, capable of having a very strong influence on our health, happiness and daily life. What we say to ourselves will become our reality, so if the doctor has told you that your medication will make you sick then it probably will. If you watch children undergoing chemotherapy you will be amazed at the way they run around living normally – this is because they have not usually been told all of the facts and the potential hazards of the treatments. They discover and deal with the side effects as they arise rather than worrying about the future before it arrives. The children have a much better journey through their cancer because of this.

If negative thoughts are continually focused upon, feelings will follow thought and we will create our own reality. People have said that it is easy for me to do this as I appear to be a positive person, but it has not always been easy. It is like any other habit we have – we can change our patterns if we really want to and we can retrain our thoughts in time. It is not a question of never having negative thoughts, which would be unrealistic; it is more a matter of letting the negative come and go and then replacing the negative thought with a positive one. After a while this can become second nature.

When Sam was ill and I first used affirmations I used to look in the mirror, say my affirmation and think how ridiculous the whole thing was. It was the same with some of the alternative therapies we tried. However, everything is worth trying, and after a few days of doing my affirmations I couldn't look in the mirror without sobbing – I was beginning to reach the hurt and emotional pain behind the cheerful face that I wore to please other people. If we can release our emotional pain we can have a positive effect on our physical body and life.

A useful thing to remember is that affirmations are not a statement of intent – you must phrase them in the present tense. If you are ill and you say, 'I will be well', your health may well stay just out of reach. However if you say, 'I *am* well', then hopefully that will become your reality. Certainly, when things started to improve for me I went from feeling silly to beginning to respect the tool I was using.

The subconscious is a willing tool. It has probably been used to you feeding negative messages into it for many years, and will take time to accept these new positive messages. But if you persist it will respond, and the benefits will be felt on many levels.

Another powerful tool we can use is the releasing letter, to express your emotions (I did this to resolve angry feeling towards my father). To write a love letter, begin by expressing your anger and resentment and then allow yourself to move through the other levels such as hurt and sadness, fear and insecurity, guilt and responsibility until you get down to love and forgiveness and understanding. Behind most anger there is love. However, if you simply write to someone and unload all your baggage, you may get an angry or very confused response. If you word the letter in a non-confrontational way – ending with love – it will have a very different effect. Some of my clients prefer not to post these letters, preferring to burn them instead, and that's fine – just writing them in itself is powerful self-healing.

One of my greatest pleasures is working with children. As I've said, it is for me very similar to healing on animals in that the children are very open to energy. This, I feel, is because their minds have not developed the ability to mask their feelings. I will often say to my adult clients that I would like them to be more childlike, to say what they feel, instead of hiding their feelings and letting them fester inside.

Children's negative feelings are very much on the surface, which makes them far easier to work with. The expression, 'Out of the mouths of babes and children' is very accurate; there is very little pretence in a child or an animal. A child's anger or happiness is clearly seen on their faces, sometimes all within the same five minutes!

Children do sometimes hide their feelings; to protect their parents, for instance. I found Alex (the little bear) invaluable with Sam, but any inanimate object will fulfil the same purpose of sharing difficult feelings.

The Alex-time sessions I had with Sam would take the following format (I would answer in a 'bear-type' voice for Alex as he didn't speak English!). Be warned, your child will soon find you out if you are not honest, but it is up to you how honest you want to be. Do not question what your child tells you, and do not make comment on anything that is said. Sam and I would do this every night. Sometimes it would be a quick run-through, but often we would spend many hours talking and hooting with laughter. Occasionally one or the other of us would become tearful as we both released our feelings, and of course every session ended with a big cuddle.

Another way of releasing frustrated feelings that we both enjoyed was to draw a picture of the person's face that had annoyed us and then stick it to a pillow. Then beat up the pillow! Very satisfying and it usually ended up in a fit of the giggles.

When a child comes for healing I will usually explain what I am going to do in energy terms similar to *E.T.* or, lately, *Harry Potter* – the idea of energy being transferred between people is demonstrated in both these films. They are usually very happy to jump on the healing couch or, if not, they can sit on a parent's lap. The healing session is much shorter, maybe twenty minutes maximum, and the children usually giggle a lot as they feel the energy 'tickling their insides'. I give them a small crystal to take home with them which I ask them to place under their pillows and cleanse under a tap in the morning when they wake. This continues the healing work.

Although children are very easy for me to work with, I never forget that children often act as sponges for negativity within a family and will sometimes be holding a lot of anger within their bodies. This very rarely needs to be talked about, but their bodies will react very strongly to the energy, causing twitching in their hands and feet as the negative emotions are cleared away.

Some children are very developed 'old souls', and these are the children who will often have an imaginary friend. I believe these children are seeing spirit children, but unfortunately they will often be told 'not to be so silly' and will lose the ability to 'see' these spirit children as they grow up. There is no mistaking these 'old souls', as they have wisdom far beyond their years.

One such child (aged seven) had taken a lot of interest in my healing room when he first came to see me, and asked a lot of questions about Sam, whose picture hangs on the wall. The little boy questioned me closely about where the energy was coming from, and I gave him my usual explanation, that is that some people believe it comes from the universe, some people believe it comes from Jesus or God, and some believe that it comes from a person we know who is in heaven. I looked at this beautiful child and asked him if he knew where mine was coming from. He replied, 'Well, it's Sam of course.' Who am I to argue with him?

Children need fewer appointments to help them than adults. Two or three sessions are usually sufficient and then I tell them to call me at any time if they need further help. I have children who I have seen for several years but only on an annual basis after their problem has cleared up. It is lovely to see them grow up without whatever affliction brought them to me in the first place.

Many children are being attuned to Reiki at the present time and attending meditation groups. I have been very happy to read articles recently that some enlightened schools are offering meditation sessions to their pupils. This can only help them as they become more caring to each other and calmer generally. There are a few meditation books available which give meditations for children and if your child is open to the idea you will find it a loving thing to do together, perhaps instead of the usual bedtime story.

Most children's ailments can benefit from healing, and my advice would be to approach a healer who is used to working with children and who you know has a good reputation. There are various bodies within the UK that hold a register of healers who will be able to give you the contact details of a healer in your area (see the resources section at the back). Ring the healer to check their credentials and experience. It is important that you like the sound of the person to whom you are taking your child for healing. It goes without saying that you should never leave your child alone with anyone you do not know and trust.

If your child is unfortunate enough to have cancer, do not despair. As my own story hopefully shows, there are many things that you can do to help yourself and your child, as well as taking the best that modern medicine can offer.

In hindsight I believe the most useful things we used for Sam were the herbal drink Essiac, the healing, keeping active and having fun whenever possible. However, your child is an individual and you should be guided by him or her as far as possible.

CHAPTER 36

Some of the alternative therapies available to you might be a little confusing. Hopefully my story has explained many of them, but the following pages offer a list of more of the tried and tested tools that helped Sam but have also helped many hundreds of my patients since Sam's passing. Again, my advice is to explore which ones you feel most drawn to and do not feel guilty if some of the tools are not for you – just go with the ones you feel you can benefit from.

MEDITATION AND VISUALISATION

There is so much help to be gained for oneself from meditation and visualisation. It can be very useful to get a friend to record a meditation for you, and then you can fully relax and just listen to a tape. If you are not confident meditating on your own, look for group meditations run by an experienced facilitator.

HEALING

There are many different types of healing treatments available to us. Indeed there are so many, it can be confusing for the patient to choose which route to take.

Spiritual healing, Reiki and therapeutic touch are all, to me, essentially energy tools. As I have said, there are guidelines for choosing a therapist written by the Royal College of Nursing which will help you. However it is a relatively simple thing these days to go on a healing course and come away with a certificate, so be less guided by certificates and more by the healer's experience. I personally feel that to be good at anything, whether you are a concert pianist, a footballer, an artist or indeed a healer, you need to practise and then work with your craft.

I am always more comfortable if someone has studied just one or two alternative therapies rather than a large number, because I believe, though I may be wrong, that they are more likely to be proficient at the couple they have learned and honed rather than being a jack of all trades.

Ask yourself two questions. How does your healer present his or herself? Are you happy and relaxed in their company? There are several registers within the UK and I list a couple at the end of the book, but even when accessing a healer via this route please ask what experience they have. When you have found a healer that you are happy with remember to look for little improvements as well as the bigger ones that you are hoping for. It might be something as simple as a child regaining an appetite or sleeping well again, or an increased ability to communicate with your loved ones that will make a difference to your life. Big improvements are possible but don't give up if the miracle takes a little longer!

ABSENT HEALING
There are many absent healing books kept around the world in places of worship or in healing sanctuaries. I have listed a couple of places where you can request healing at the back of the book. Some people believe that we all have our own guardian angel that is there to help us. Never be afraid to ask – my belief is that the angels can only help us if we ask. The trick then is to listen to the answer.

Here are a few ways to help you be aware of the answers that may come your way.

- You may dream vividly and wake up with a clear understanding of what needs to be done
- You may be listening to the radio and hear someone speaking on a subject that can help you
- You bump into an old friend whom you have not seen for years and you receive the advice you need

- Many people I have spoken to find a single white feather in their house – one friend even found one in an airport departure lounge (she was terrified of flying)
- I have been in bookshops and have books fall off the shelves in front of me!

Once you have been given the sign, it's up to you to action it. This is where 'free will' comes in.

PRAYER

There have been many studies that have proved that those patients who are prayed for do better than those who are not, even if the patient is unaware of it. (Perhaps this is another form of absent healing – if enough people are thinking about any one individual then there is an improvement in that person's condition.) I was recently watching a television programme that demonstrated this in a most miraculous way.

A woman, who had been diagnosed with bone cancer some years previously, had been successfully treated with an amputation to bring the cancer under control. Unfortunately she had relapsed.

It was an unacceptable route to have further amputation so she and her family decided to ask their church to pray for her. Eventually other churches and their congregations joined in until there were thousands of people praying for her health to be restored.

After some weeks the woman had a scan that showed the tumour had shrunk. Months later another scan was taken, as the woman was now feeling very well despite the prognosis. Amazingly, the tumour had completely disappeared and the woman remains well to this day. There is no doubt in the woman's mind that she had been healed by the power of prayer. So, if you believe that prayer will help you, don't let anyone put you off trying. I believed that it was right to try anything that might help and I would do the same again.

MUSIC

As I have said, I use music during my healing sessions; energy and music together form a very powerful combination for healing. Music alone can have wonderful effects on the mind and therefore the body. Music can do many things:

- Lift our mood
- Help us to sleep
- Create the right mood to meditate
- Put us in touch with our feelings
- Connect us to our loved ones in spirit
- Connect us to a happy or sad time in our lives, via our emotions

When I was young I would deliberately choose sad tunes to make me cry if I was upset over a boyfriend. Likewise I would put upbeat music on when it was time to move on.

LAUGHTER

I love it when my clients laugh. It is not just the children who laugh during their treatments, adults have done so as well. It is usually because their 'inner child' has been ignored and suppressed for so long that the sense of relief that healing gives them results in laughter, quickly followed by tears. As with music, laughter affects our moods and those around us. If we want to laugh we watch amusing programmes and if we want to cry we do the opposite. Laughter is the best medicine, it stimulates the immune system and is infectious to those around us.

EXERCISE

I remember when Sam was in Great Ormond Street Hospital and we were waiting for his new bone marrow to work and for his blood count to recover. We were getting increasingly frustrated and worried with each passing day when our consultant told us that the marrow would respond to exercise. Sam immediately got on the exercise bike that was in our room and pedalled for several minutes, many times a day. Within a very short time his marrow began to recover. I have seen over and over again that the patients who lie in bed do less well than those who force themselves to get up, even if it is only for short periods.

Even if you are forced to lie in bed, because you feel so weak, you can still exercise your body by moving hands and feet, and then your arms and legs. The moment you are well enough, get up! A number of studies on animals have shown that when animals are stressed and are not permitted a physical outlet for this stress, their physical bodies deteriorate. However, if the animals that are stressed are allowed to physically act, the amount of damage is minimal. Start with a small amount of exercise and work up to an hour, three times weekly. You will feel the benefit and have a much improved quality of life.

ESSIAC

Essiac is a combination of herbs that were first prepared as part of a ritual by the Ojibway Indians. The formula was given to a Canadian nurse called Rene Caisse in 1922 and became known as the Essiac tonic (Essiac is Caisse spelled backwards). Rene used this tonic on many of her patients who were suffering from cancer or other degenerative diseases and noticed remarkable improvements in their health. The formula has traditionally been used to increase the health of degenerated tissues by supporting the body's own ability to effectively remove toxins and fluid wastes from the body.

The ingredients are Burdock Root, Sheep's Sorrel Leaf, Slippery Elm Bark and Turkey Rhubarb Root. There are many anecdotal stories about the use of Essiac. Of course, you must check with your own consultant if you are intending to use it, to make sure that they are OK with it being combined with whatever traditional routes you are following, but many cancer patients and liver patients have benefited from its use with the full knowledge of the medics in charge of their care. There are many sources of Essiac, and you can access a lot of information via the Internet. I have found the source listed at the back of this book to be one of the purist.

You *must* consult with your doctor, but if you show them the components that make up Essiac, it is hard to imagine that they could have any objections.

CHAPTER 37

One of the first questions a patient will often ask me will be, 'Do you have to believe in healing for it to work?' My experience to date has been that you do not have to believe in healing or indeed have any particular belief for healing to be effective. I have found that 'labels' can be a block to people agreeing to a treatment.

My ID at the hospital states 'spiritual healer' and a lot of people assume this means I am religious. In fact, I am sitting on the fence as far as religion goes. I believe that someone named Jesus lived some time ago and was a great prophet of his time and, if we believe the stories written, a wonderful healer. However, there have been many great prophets, and I am open in my own beliefs. If someone had said to me that I would see a patient 'levitate' with my own eyes, I would have laughed at them. Now I know better, but that's because I have *seen* it for myself.

At heart I am one of the great sceptics, but the fact is I have seen many things that defy science and all that my previously logical brain would have believed possible. So when a patient says to me, 'I don't want any spiritual healing', I will respond with, 'Well, would you like some Reiki healing, then?' They will usually happily agree to this, as for most people Reiki does not have any religious connotations attached to it.

In fact, for me, whatever I call it, the treatment is exactly the same. I have studied with the National Federation of Spiritual Healers and I am also a Reiki Master. I take the best of what I have learned from both systems, add a dash of intuition and a great deal of clinical experience, resulting in what I laughingly refer to as an Angie Buxton-King special!

People seem more than happy with that and I am happy with the results of the healing. Of course, I always want more for my patients as indeed I wanted more for my son Sam. The reality is that some people get well despite the most terrible odds, and some people die despite everything, whether it is the best of conventional medicine, alternative medicine or a mixture of both. It is not all right for our children, young adults, mothers and fathers to die too young, but the fact is that everybody is going to die sometime – it is the manner of our dying that is important. Sam passed away at home having enjoyed a quality of life that was an inspiration to all who met him, and passing into spirit as he did at home was a fitting way to go. Many people die in a hospital surrounded by life-support machines and medical equipment that can rob the family of what can be the most peaceful of experiences. To die in fear is one of the greatest tragedies, and to be able to take away a patient's fear of dying is something very special that healing can offer if the patient and their families wish.

I am often asked questions about the other side of life and the spiritual world, and thanks to the messages I receive I feel I have some idea of what happens when we die. I have not experienced it for myself and, until I do, anything I say is only my belief system; you do not necessarily have to accept it unless it feels right for you.

I believe that when we die it is our essence (or spirit or personality) that lives on. Our essence separates from our physical body as we make the transition from this realm to the next. This essence vibrates at a much faster rate than we do in the physical world, but is just as real.

I believe that we are then met by familiar faces and loved ones who have gone before us. My belief is that a spirit person looks the same as a physical person but, because they are vibrating at a higher rate, they will appear as light bodies. The spirit world is all around us but because of the higher frequency/vibration we cannot see it unless we have the ability to raise our vibration as a medium does. Think of what happens if you sit and look at an electric fan. The blades are rotating so quickly that they become invisible to the human eye, but they are there just the same – and if your brain could process images quickly enough you would be able to see them.

It is a similar process to be able to see the spirit world, but unfortunately most of us do not have the ability to raise our vibration to do this and to be able to see our loved ones. In the same way, if you have experienced a thought that seems to have come from nowhere, I believe it will most likely have come from your loved ones in spirit who are trying to help you in some way.

Because of my beliefs, I feel it is just as important to communicate with our loved ones after they have passed into spirit, and here are a few ideas as to how to do this.

- Speak their name naturally, in conversation. This will let them know that you are aware they still exist and maintain the bond with them.
- Act naturally. Contact is often felt when we are doing simple chores and thinking about nothing in particular. This is often the gap in our usually active minds that our loved ones can imprint a telepathic message upon.
- Be aware of their presence – a familiar smell, perfume or tobacco, for instance.
- Acknowledge their presence when you feel it by a simple 'Hello' or 'I love you'. Many spirits will be able to affect electrical equipment; for example, equipment will stop and not restart or lights will flicker on and off.

I was on holiday in Rhodes recently when Graham and I decided to visit a monastery dedicated to archangel Michael.

In 1995, the year Sam was diagnosed with leukaemia, I had visited a similar monastery on the island of Cyprus. On that occasion Sam and I lit a candle for my mother, who had passed into spirit some years previously. There were many candles lit that day in Cyprus, and while we were placing ours a monk came out from behind a curtain and blew out all the candles except the ones that

Sam and I had placed there. A chill ran through me, but I made a joke about it to Sam and we left the church. In hindsight I think it was a sign of the hard times to come.

Now, many years later, I was lighting candles again, and as I did so I sent out a thought to Sam to please give me some sort of sign that he was still around me. I left the candles and walked down the church to sit quietly in a pew.

After a few moments a monk came into the church and began to blow out the candles. I watched him from where I sat and began to feel the hairs on the back of my neck tingle as the monk blew all the candles out except the one I had lit for Sam. He picked up the remaining candle, walked down the church and stopped in front of the icon of mother and child. Then he lit the oil lamp that illuminated the special icon with the candle I had lit. I felt such a rush of love and energy flow through my body and mentally thanked Sam for giving me my own very special sign.

POSTSCRIPT

So what has it all been about, this journey that I and my family have experienced? Some people would have us believe that it was all for a reason. I personally find this a belief that is very hard to subscribe to. Many of us who have lost our loved ones struggle to find a reason for the death of a child, a mother or beloved partner.

Of course, I would rather have Sam back with me, healthy and happy, and for our family never to have experienced all that we have. But the unthinkable did happen, Sam developed leukaemia for whatever reason (our consultant said the odds were equivalent to two children per year in a city the size of Manchester) and, as a consequence of this, we as a family lived with the situation, and did our best. That is all any of us can ever do.

Along the way I discovered strengths within my own child that inspired and astounded me. In our search for health for Sam, I discovered many different ways to help him and to help myself. Some of these I value greatly and I now have a greater understanding of many things than I did before. His strength and his inspiration are, I believe, his gift to me and to many others. If it weren't for him I would never have taken my healing to the lengths to which I have, and I would never have worked at UCLH and become the only paid healer within the NHS.

I have had so much proof that Sam's spirit still lives that I cannot do anything other that 'walk the walk' and get on with my life until we are reunited. Despite this, the loss of his physical self still catches me unawares at times and I find myself plunged back into grief as if it were yesterday. I believe this is completely normal and something we all, in some way or another, have to walk with when we have lost someone we love.

Nick has grown into a fine young man; despite all that he has experienced, he has grown into a caring, sensitive man of whom I am very proud. David has moved on in his own life and has a new relationship that supports him and gives him the love that he deserves.

In fact we have all survived, although at times I doubted that we would. Graham and I are very lucky to have found each other. We are each strong individuals who have common goals, we both believe in healing and are mutually supportive of each other. I know that we will achieve more together than we ever could have done separately.

Many of the patients that I have mentioned are alive and healthy, while some of them are in spirit – 'home and free' – but I will never forget any of them. Every year we hold a Christmas party at UCLH for our ex-patients. It is wonderful to meet up with people who you have known in the worst moments of their lives and find you cannot recognise them because they look so well. They have a full head of hair and healthy complexions, quite often unrecognisable to us if we have not seen them for a while.

This year I met up with several who said again that the healing they received played an important part in their fight to be well again. One patient, Don, said that he had recently had a scare as his blood tests showed his marrow was once again failing. The doctors had told him to go home and put his affairs in order.

Instead he went home, ate well, took long bike rides and decided that he wasn't ready to die yet; his blood tests now show a more optimistic outlook.

Don said to me that he thought of what I had said to him when he was in hospital and it seemed there was no hope of a recovery: 'Anything's possible, Don. Just live each day', and so he did.

I want many things for the future. One of my reasons for writing this book is to touch other people with the knowledge that there are many things that we can do to help ourselves and our families, no matter what the problem, and that there are many avenues of help available to us. I have tried to show you that in the absence of anything else, there is nothing wrong with hope; hope is the lifeblood of humanity and without it we are truly lost.

I have come from having suicidal thoughts in the depths of my despair, to arriving at a point in my life where I have never been stronger, and I look forward to the future and whatever it has in store for me. You can, too, whatever your circumstances.

This book has focused on healing people and animals that are already sick, but I would like us to have a shift in our understanding of health and recognise that healing can also be used as preventative medicine. In this hectic world that we live in it is hard to achieve the balance that we need to stay healthy. It is not enough to practise 'reactive medicine'; we should be looking at preventative medicine in a more holistic way than just considering our diets and what recreational poisons we put into our bodies.

It is a goal of mine to spread the therapy of healing within hospitals, not on a voluntary basis, but as a valued part of an integrated team, as I am at UCLH, which offers the patients the holistic care that they need.

I hope in the future to create a Healing Sanctuary in Sam's name so that anybody who needs help will know that there is a place for them to come and spend time to heal their mind, body and spirit. The sanctuary will offer healing, of course, but there will also be a wide range of other therapies available so that people do not have to search as I did for ways to help their child or loved one. I want the sanctuary to be without religion but with all belief systems represented, so that all creeds and colours will feel at home and welcomed.

There needs to be a greater awareness that healing on a hospital ward requires different skills from the ones than are currently being taught by any healing organisation. It is a hard environment to work in, as hospitals are science-based and healing is not understood by science yet. Every time I enter a room on the ward I am asked to validate what I do, and it has been a period of great personal growth as I have struggled with my old patterns of fear of rejection.

I have learned to stand in my own light and let the healing do the talking. When I am judged, I ask to be judged by the results achieved and felt by my patients and I have been fortunate to find that my employers at UCLH have done just that. To help healers be effective in this hard environment I intend to run courses at the sanctuary to pass on the hard-earned knowledge that will stand them in good stead.

For myself, I now look forward to the future and wherever my journey will take me next. I know I will never be alone. Before Sam passed into spirit we said to each other that if we should ever become separated, he would sit on my shoulder and I would be on his. I have been given so much proof that this is truly so – Sam was the reason that I am where I am today and I look forward to whatever way the healing will take me. Since this book was written, Ron Moulding, my great friend and spiritual mentor, has also passed into spirit. I will miss his physical presence enormously but look forward to hearing from him in the future.

For the moment I hope to continue with my work at the hospital, while also seeing my private patients at home. I have always been happy to raise my head up above the parapet ready to be shot at. If we want the benefits of healing to spread, we have to speak our truth, hence my appearance on *Kilroy* and other programmes. Even if we only reach one person, that person has benefited and it has all been worthwhile.

RESOURCES

Angie Buxton-King
PO Box 989
Hemel Hempstead
HP3 8YQ
08450 738883
www.angiebuxton-king.com
angel.beacon@virgin.net

The Beacon of Healing Light
Angie and Graham King
PO Box 989
Hemel Hempstead
HP3 8YQ
08450 738883
angel.beacon@virgin.net
Healing appointments – Reiki treatments – Reiki attunements –
Meditation groups – Self-development classes – Animal healing –
Absent healing – Courses

Harry Edwards Healing Sanctuary
Burrows Lea
Shere
Guildford
Surrey
GU5 9QG

01483 202054
Absent healing

National Federation of Spiritual Healers
Old Manor Farm Studios
Church Street
Sunbury-on-Thames
Middlesex
TW16 6RJ
01932 783164/5
Courses for healing and healing referral line

UK Reiki Federation
PO Box 1785
Andover
Hants
SP11 OWB
01264 773774
www.reikifed.co.uk
Register of Reiki practitioners
Mediums
Eva O'Brien
01279 436277

Paulene Carey
01707 266183

Shirley West
01462 623044

Spiritualist Association of Great Britain
33 Belgrave Square
London
SW1X 8QB
020 7235 3351

Jacqui Beacon and David Gillet
Environmental Harmony
PO Box 3912
London
NW11 6AZ
www.enviromental-harmony.com
Environmental stress – Courses

Doctor–Healer Network
27 Montefiore Court
Stamford Hill
London
N16 5TY
020 8800 3569
Network for doctors and healers who work side by side

Peter Clifford
The Phoenix Foundation
PO Box 1305
Sudbury
Suffolk
CO10 0UA
Email: phoenixfound@btinternet.com
Flower remedies – Courses

Sara Goldman
Fundraiser LALU
University College Hospital NHS Trust
Room 401
4th Floor
Grafton Way
London
WC1E 6AU
Email: sara.goldman@uclh.org

Essiac Source
The Herbalist
2106 NE 65th Street
Seattle
WA 98115
USA
Tel: (001 206) 523 2600

RECOMMENDED READING

Hay, Louise L., *You Can Heal Your Life,* Eden Grove Editions, 1995.

Siegel, Bernie, MD, *Love, Medicine and Miracles,* Random House (Arrow), 1989.

Stein, Diane, *Essential Reiki: A Complete Guide to an Ancient Healing Art*, Crossing Press, 1995.

Van Praagh, James, *Talking to Heaven: A Medium's Message of Life After Death*, Signet, 1999.